TOMORROW IS
D-DAY

ABOUT THE AUTHOR

Stella Rutter was educated at Southern College of Art, Portsmouth, and went on to the Experimental Drawing Office, Whale Island. She transferred to Vickers-Armstrong, the world-famous designer of the Spitfire, where she found herself to be the only girl among male draughtsmen. In retirement, Stella was appointed as the first Chairman of the Central Region of the Spitfire Society in the initial year of its formation. She has kept in close contact with the Spitfire Society ever since. On 22 May 1999 Air Marshal Sir Ivor Broom awarded Stella the honour of being a member of the RAF Association in recognition of her work for Supermarine and she has attended their meetings to date. She lives in Hampshire.

TOMORROW IS
D-DAY

STELLA RUTTER

AMBERLEY

This book is a tribute to all my colleagues who worked so diligently throughout the war at Supermarine. As a civilian myself I have been privileged to meet and talk with senior commanders of D-Day, being fully aware of the extreme security required and the necessity of keeping shtum.

This edition first published 2015

Amberley Publishing
The Hill, Stroud
Gloucestershire, GL5 4EP

www.amberley-books.com

Copyright © Stella Rutter, 2014, 2015

The right of Stella Rutter to be identified as the Author of this work has been asserted in accordance with the Copyrights, Designs and Patents Act 1988.

ISBN 978 1 4456 4722 7 (paperback)
ISBN 978 1 4456 3303 9 (ebook)

British Library Cataloguing in Publication Data. A catalogue record for this book is available from the British Library.

Typesetting and Origination by Amberley Publishing
Printed in the UK.

CONTENTS

The following lines inspired me throughout the war and I have endeavoured to keep these precepts before me throughout my life:

This royal throne of kings, this sceptred isle,
This earth of majesty, this seat of Mars,
This other Eden, demi-paradise,
This fortress built by Nature for herself
Against infection and the hand of war,
This happy breed of men, this little world,
This precious stone set in the silver sea,
Which serves it in the office of a wall
Or as a moat defensive to a house
Against the envy of less happier lands, –
This blessed plot, this earth, this realm, this England.

William Shakespeare, *King Richard II*, Act 2 scene 1

FOREWORD FROM THE EARL OF GAINSBOROUGH

I was delighted when Stella invited me to provide a foreword for this fascinating book on her life and times from when she worked in the Drawing Office at Vickers Supermarine – as I did myself.

The Drawing Office comprised many sections. My section was relatively near to Stella, divided by an aisle. Social discussion between employees was not encouraged during working hours. Most people knew Stella, who was a striking-looking young woman with a strong personality, and her section was known by many as 'The Special Branch'. Gerry Gingell, her section leader, on entering Supermarine as a young man in the design staff, worked with the legendary designer R. J. Mitchell until his demise prior to the Second World War, when he was succeeded by Joseph Smith, who became the Chief Designer.

Stella told me many years later of the special task she had undertaken involving a top-security meeting leading up to the invasion of Europe in 1944 by Allied forces on D-Day. Present were senior British military commanders, including Major Generals D.

A. H. Graham, Rodney Keller, Thomas Rennie and Richard Gale, and the American commanders Lieutenant General Omar Bradley and Major General Clarence Huebner.

At the conclusion of the war, most of us went our own ways, and it was many years before Stella and I met again. This was a special occasion at the Southampton Museum of Aviation. Jeffrey Quill, one of the two Supermarine chief test pilots, desired that a book should be produced recording all the people who were associated with the development of the Spitfire and Seafire aircraft. I had the privilege of being one of the signatories, although the part I played was of a very junior nature. Stella is also included under her maiden name of Broughton.

Since then I have remained in touch with Stella, who has become a real friend. As more than sixty years have elapsed since we both worked together at Hursley Park, memories are not quite as good as they were, but I certainly remember Stella, as will all the rest of the staff who knew her, many of whom, sadly, are no longer with us. I am sure all those who read this book will be amazed at its remarkable contents and she deserves every success in the publication of her book.

5th Earl of Gainsborough, 2007

FOREWORD FROM AIR MARSHAL SIR DUSTY MILLER

Many have seen the film *Saving Private Ryan* and are thus able to imagine the true horror of an invasion of strongly defended territory. In the opening scenes the film captures with graphic clarity the awfulness of the whole enterprise, leaving the viewer to reflect on the incredible courage of those who gave everything in order for Europe to start moving along the path towards freedom.

What is not captured is the weight of responsibility borne by the political and military leaders who made the decision that 'tomorrow is D-Day' – the decision that pitched many thousands of young men into the seething cauldron of the Normandy beaches, which eventually led to Europe breaking free from the yoke of Nazism. Here, the decision over when to attack was very different to the decisions related to defence; in the latter case, the enemy had already set the timing. In the former, leaders will always question whether or not sufficient preparation has been made: Have we trained to meet, and thought through most thoroughly, all possible outcomes? Are we able to support with food, ammunition and medical care our committed forces, come what may? Are the weather conditions at their most suitable? Will our deception plans fool the enemy?

In this book, Stella Rutter gives a very clear insight into many of the men who either contributed to or made the gravest decision that 'tomorrow is D-Day'. She puts to work her exceptional powers of recall to give the reader a very clear picture of the commanders she met on the evening of Saturday 3 June 1944 who, perhaps feeling some measure of self-doubt, nevertheless summoned the courage that ultimately led to us being free to live as we do today. Stella writes with a captivating and compelling style that I hope you will enjoy reading – I know I did.

Air Marshal Sir Dusty Miller

PREFACE

W hat an extraordinary thing! I feel as though I am watching a play and yet I am one of the players. Not two minutes ago my usually placid father burst into the kitchen calling for Mother to come and see. Being curious, I followed her down the hall and out of the front door. They were both looking up into the sky. There, hovering as any galleon of old, was an enormous silver-grey airship, not more than 100 feet above the houses opposite.

'What is it?' I gasped.

'It's a dirigible,' said Father.

A droning noise came from it, penetrating our senses and drowning all other sounds. I could see a swastika in red and black on the tail plane and the name 'Hindenburg' was on the side. The faces of officers and passengers could be seen looking down at us through the windows, and it was weird and very frightening. Slowly it pivoted to follow the coastal road and disappeared towards Cosham.

Father turned and looked at me with such sad eyes and said quietly, 'We are seeing the beginning of a new era. It means that anyone can fly over land or sea.' Being an astute man he further commented forcefully, 'The Channel is no longer a barrier. Now, no one is safe.' He went into the house. Shocked, I turned to Mother for some explanation, but she brushed past me as though I was invisible, calling out, 'Charles, what do you mean?' and followed him into the drawing room, closing the door behind her.

Never had I known such isolation. It was unheard of for me to be left unattended outside the front door! Closing the front door, hearing no sounds – not even talking – I crept back indoors. Eventually, when Mother returned to the kitchen, the look on her face caused me to refrain from making any reference to such unusual behaviour. The sound lingered in the air like a magic spell, but something remained – an elusive yearning for the unknown. My parents would never understand my fascination with the feel of speed in space.

The following year, May 1937, the *Hindenburg* left Berlin on a flight to the USA. It was delayed by headwinds and as it approached Lakehurst it was forced to circle the aerodrome and wait for a thunderstorm to clear. As it neared the mooring mast, the airship suddenly burst into flames. This horrific accident was viewed by the relatives and friends of the passengers, and a live broadcast by a reporter relayed the tragic event to the world.

Years later I realised that Father, having experienced raids by Zeppelins in the First World War, had seen that this flight of the *Hindenburg* showed the probability of the German Air Force being able to bomb cities throughout the British Isles. He knew that the English Channel was no longer our first line of defence. How right he was.

In Bedford one day in May 1990, I heard this same droning noise. Looking out of my window I saw the dirigible from Cardington floating serenely past, and the story above came flooding back into my mind.

1

STELLA'S ROAD TO WAR

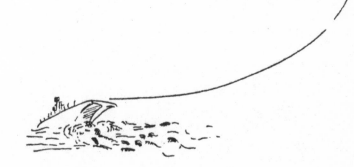

I was born on 15 September 1923 at 9.15 a.m. A photograph taken by Papa of me in Nurse's arms at a week old shows lots of black hair and a screwed-up expression, probably resenting having been taken out in the sunshine. Shortly afterwards I was christened at the Congregational church in Havant as Joyce Isabel Stella, the fourth child of Charles Henry and Isabel Nora Broughton. In my early years I answered to the name of Joyce, but changed to being called Stella on entering Purbrook Park County High School.

My birthday, 15 September, is memorable and significant because it marks Battle of Britain Day. From early years it had some influence on my life, for instance, my interest in flight and involvement in the forces. Also born that year were personalities who became famous in the fields of theatre and film, namely Sir Richard Attenborough, Charlton Heston and Marcel Marceau. Is it any wonder I have had a great interest in drama? Shortly after my birth, the Nazi Party held its first rally in Munich, eventually bringing Adolf Hitler into power for the next two decades.

I was brought up in a strict Edwardian atmosphere where young children under the age of five were in the care of Nanny, and were taught to be seen and not heard in adult company. As a result of this upbringing, I was able to cope at a very early age with social situations and the intricacies of etiquette. At her meetings, Mother would tell me to hand around the teacakes and not to repeat anything I heard. Older children, up to the age of twenty-one, were expected to defer to their parents' wishes regardless of their own inclinations.

For my first three years Mama was a remote person, as I was put in the charge of Nanny, who regulated my life. On Wednesday, Nanny's half day, she would dress me after lunch in my second-best dress and take me down to the dining room. Placing me on the rug in front of the fire with my doll, she bid me play quietly until Mama had finished writing letters at her desk in the alcove. Then Mama took me out to walk to the postbox. On our return we had tea and then she put me to bed.

A naturally obedient child, I had an inquisitive disposition, an enquiring mind and wanted to know how this or that was done – and why! I must have driven Mother to distraction in my quest for knowledge. Any snippets of family news, overheard while pretending not to hear, were stored in my memory, especially those which appeared to be fraught with unexplained meanings. Sometimes when I asked what was being spoken about I would be told to be quiet, or not to be forward, or, worst of all, stared at and frozen into silence.

What a set down for the enquiring mind – but it was good training in keeping my mouth shut and my ears open in order to learn matters of which I was not supposed to know anything. Little did my parents know what a service they did me, or how useful this trait was to be in my future life.

We moved to number 14 Bedhampton Hill, named 'Speedfield', on the north side of Bedhampton Hill, in 1926. 'Speedfield' was a semi-detached mid-nineteenth-century house which had a communal driveway to the rear of the property, between the two semi-detached houses. Inside, the front rooms were separated from the domestic quarters by an inner hall and stairwell. A huge bookcase with carved edges, 6 feet high and 6 feet wide, stood on the upstairs landing before the door, which separated the rear bedrooms from the front of the house. A massive mirror, gilt framed, hung from floor to ceiling between this door and the three steps up to the main corridor. In the rear corridor there were two large cupboards, and these held Mother's stock of Christmas puddings, jars of preserves, tins and other dry goods for which there was no room in the kitchen. A perfect layout for an Edwardian family. I saw very little of Father as a general rule. But on every Saturday morning as I was eating my breakfast at the kitchen table he would roll up his sleeves and slip on the metal bracelets to keep them up above his elbows, sit down on the shoebox and while tying his shoelaces would sing musical ditties to amuse me. One of his favourites was:

She was a sweet little dicky bird, Tweet, Tweet, Tweet she went
Sweetly she sang to me 'til all my money was spent.
Then she went off song, we parted on fighting terms
She was one of the early birds, and I was one of the worms.

And another was:

Down the road went Polly with a step so jolly that I knew she'd win.
The pace was killing tho' the mare was willing for a lightening spin.
All the rest were licked and might as well ne'er been born
Whoa mare, whoa mare, you've earnt your little bit of corn.

At which Mother would call from the kitchen with the admonition 'Charles!' He would stop mid-stream, but with a wink continued in a whisper. It was only on these occasions I saw his eyes twinkle, otherwise his demeanour was always unruffled. His maxim was 'Everything in moderation'. Adding a soft cap and a jacket, he would be ready for work. The plan for each Saturday had been decided beforehand, and he always arranged the delivery of whatever was required well in advance, which meant that no time was wasted.

When I was six years old Mother decreed that on Saturday mornings I was to help Father and my brothers by being a 'go for'. This was one way of getting me out from under her feet. At eleven o'clock she would call me to carry the 'elevenses' out to them. My portion, the top of a cottage loaf buttered and a chunk of cheese with a cup of cocoa in the open air, in every month of the year, was memorable.

At every opportunity during these sessions, I listened and watched Father explaining to my brothers the use of brushes, the right way to hang wallpaper, paint, and repair casements and windows with putty. Father was particular about handling tools, and I was very privileged to be allowed to use his chisels when I was eight years old. Outside, I absorbed the information of proportions required for cement laying, the way to build brick walls and erect the timber construction for a roof. In the garden, potatoes and vegetables were planted and fruit trees pruned. Against the south wall loganberries grew in profusion. In front of them Mother planted *Leucojums* and the short species of *Crocosmia*, known as montbretia, believed to be the flower symbol of her family.

Outside the back door was a brick washhouse. Dark-leaved periwinkle bordered the three steps that led to the level of the garden. At the rear of the washhouse facing the garden was the outside privy, screened by green-painted lattice to conceal the wooden seat. In the summer it was a pleasant enough place, but in the winter it was very cold and dark, in spite of a small lamp. The privy was later removed and Father built upwards to create an upstairs loft, accessible by a ladder. A tiled roof and a skylight were inserted, and a large window facing the garden swung open to give access for timber and goods to be stored. This loft extended to the house wall and on to the outside wall of the drive. Between this wall and the wash house a flush toilet was installed. In the remaining open space behind the toilet my box swing was hung from a hook so I could watch Mother hanging out the washing out of the wind, and it became my secret place.

Somewhere, I think it may have been from a Naval source, Father managed to buy a couple of ships' masts. These were set in concrete 3 feet deep along the garden path. Pulleys were attached at three levels on the masts and on the washhouse. The very best woven rope was purchased and threaded through the pulleys to form a washing line. A short piece left over was bound at each end and became my skipping rope.

When all three lines were full of sheets the line took on the aspect of a ship in full sail. Mother could wash blankets in the morning, turn them at lunchtime, and they would be aired enough to put back on the beds by the evening. Quite a feat in those days. Over the next five years, every Saturday and most of the holidays were devoted to decorating and installing electric lights in the rest of the house. Special paint was used to cover the outside concrete facing of the house. Our bicycles were stored under cover when the veranda was glassed in.

In the scullery a corner unit housed the copper boiler, underneath which a small fire heated the water. It was my job on Monday mornings to light this fire. This was how laundry was boiled in those days. After boiling it was rinsed in the brown sink under a water pump and put through rollers of a large hand-turned mangle outside. When the scullery was refurbished the copper boiler and the fireplace were removed. The water pump was taken out and a deep white Bedford sink was plumbed with piped running water. Mother bought a modern mangle with rubber rollers, which was clamped on to the edge allowing the water to drain straight into the sink. It saved on time and labour – we no longer had to scoop water from the copper or drain water from the mangle outside. A full-sized bath with a wooden cover was installed against the party wall. My parents were very modern in their outlook.

Being on the main coastal road we often had tramps who knocked on our side door requesting boiling water for their billy cans. Mother often gave them a spoonful of tea and a buttered crust of bread. Gypsies would call once a year selling lace and bunches of heather. Sometimes a knife grinder would call and sharpen knives, seated on a tricycle that operated as a grinding machine. Milk was delivered from the local farm to the side door by a farmhand with a milk churn on his tricycle. At the door he would use a long-handled ladle to measure milk into our jugs.

We were very lucky to have a corner shop at the bottom of the hill owned by Mr Coleman where he sold bread, cakes, groceries and locally grown fruit and vegetables. He had a bakery behind the shop in Brookside Lane. When he bought the adjoining house he opened it as a butchers. All his meat came from the local farmer and was kept in a large refrigerator at the rear. A hole in the shop wall was made into the butcher's shop so that customers could pay for their goods directly to the cashier. This business went from strength to strength, and by 1939 it sold everything apart from milk, fish or clothes.

One night as I was being put to bed Nanny told me she was leaving the next day to look after another little girl. Yes, I did realise I was to go to school and therefore Nanny would not have to look after me during the day, and yes, I could also see she had to look after someone else. But why couldn't she still stay with us? She was *my* Nanny. No, she said sadly, she had to go too far away. Then I asked if she would come to visit me, or could I go to see her. She replied in a very quiet voice that, no, that would not be possible.

I was heartbroken. What made it worse was that I had had no warning this might happen. Nanny was my anchor, and having her torn from me left me utterly distraught, for I did not even see her the next morning to say goodbye. In fact, I do not think she even stayed the night, for her bed did not look as though it had been slept in. I felt bereft of all security. The next morning Mother came to get me up. I could not eat any breakfast and she found me inconsolable at Nanny's sudden disappearance. This state of affairs lasted a long time, and I became introspective and very wary of adults.

Shortly after Nanny left I started school. Mother bought a puppy for me to look after, but it was ill and was soon taken away. Then it was thought a kitten would be more suitable. I was taken to choose one from four pure-white half-Persian kittens that were for sale. As I sat down on the floor, one kitten with a blue ribbon made straight for me and climbed on my lap. I was enchanted. Mother wanted me to choose one with a pink ribbon, but, 'No – this one is mine.' I called him Jinky. He was my constant companion for twelve years.

My elder brother was in teacher training and happened to be taking the infants' class when I joined Bedhampton Primary School. Used to him giving me instruction at home, it was a comfortable start to school life. We had to do our lessons on slates for the first year and then we were given pencils and paper. We did not work in ink until we were nine years old. After one term he left for another school and another teacher arrived – a very kind and gentle-voiced lady.

At the age of seven I moved up into Miss Randall's class. This was not a happy experience, as during this time I encountered bullying, both mental and physical. From the age of five I suffered nearly all the childhood diseases, thereby losing valuable school time. She expected me to know what had already been taught in class. Although I did my best, I could never please her. Consequently she considered me a tiresome pupil. We had no lessons on Friday afternoon as everyone brought toys and games to exchange. For the last hour the whole school met together to learn the words and sing songs from *The National Song Book*. My favourite songs were 'The Vicar of Bray' and 'The Ash Grove'. In the summer term we had to learn 'Richmond Hill' and we had to sing this every Friday. At morning assembly we sang 'All Things Bright and Beautiful'. It became the norm to close the day with 'Now the Day is Over'.

One Tuesday in June an older girl named Cynthia insisted on giving me a piggy back. I wasn't at all keen, but I agreed to go as far as the end of the ribbon development of houses set well back from the road. Just after the last house the path went over a hill and I requested to be put down. Instead she ignored me and turned into the narrow path to the electric building edged with nettles. Here, out of sight of the road, she calmly tipped me off backwards onto the enormous bed of 4-foot-high nettles. To prevent me getting up she knelt on me pressing down on every limb. I screamed for help, but no one came to my rescue as we could not be seen due to the height of the nettles. Eventually she ran off.

The nettles had stung me through my dress, and my arms, back and legs were numb with a pain which was indescribable. It took me ages before I could muster the effort to raise myself off the crushed stems and roll over to crawl along the gravel to the grass-edged path and stand up. Instinctively my feet carried me home, past our neighbour, whom I called Aunty Scragg, without stopping. When I reached our kitchen she was but a couple of steps behind me, and I heard her say, 'Mrs Broughton, I do apologise for walking in without knocking but Joyce went by my gate and did not recognise me! What has happened?' Between them they gently removed my clothing and Mother threw a newly washed sheet over the kitchen table so that I could lie face down with my arms over the edge. Mother picked up her purse and, leaving me with Aunty, went across the road to telephone the doctor. She quite forgot to take off her pinafore!

Dr Jim Dewhurst arrived in just ten minutes, having driven from the Havant surgery a mile away. As he came through our hall I heard him say, 'Now, Mrs Broughton, what is the matter?' As he entered the kitchen I heard him exclaim 'Oh my God!' And then there was silence. He was too professional to have sworn in that manner without extreme provocation. Apologising for his outburst, he asked Mother if she had any calamine lotion, but she only had Dettol. Diluting it with cool boiled water and using cotton wool, he swabbed my body from neck to toes. While doing so he spoke to me in a consoling manner, both to distract me from the pain and to endeavour to discover who had attacked me and why. He tried to be gentle, but as there was no space between the blisters it was a painful procedure. Being in such pain I had no embarrassment at my nudity. He then gave me a tetanus injection and I think a sedative, as I can only remember being helped to lie face down on a soft bank of cushions and left without even a sheet over me, it was so painful. Dr Dewhurst took Mother with him in his car to Havant to buy calamine lotion, and Aunty was left to stay with me until she came back.

It was very late in the evening when I woke to find Father applying calamine lotion all over me. I knew he had been a first aider in the First World War and I accepted his unusual attention with equanimity. Mother told me that evening that while I had been asleep there had been a meeting between Miss Sparrow, Headmistress of Bedhampton School, Dr Dewhurst and my parents. Cynthia was to be expelled the next morning.

The next day the blisters had subsided, but my skin was very tight. Mother had to keep using the calamine lotion, which was lovely and cool, and I could sit on a soft down cushion to eat my meals. Mother told me I would have to go to school the next day. I was adamant in my refusal. If I was sent back I would run away. I would not return to that school to be subjected to Miss Randall's spite, for Cynthia had been her favourite pupil. Mother knew I meant what I said and asked, 'Where do you think you can continue your education?' I replied, 'Can't I go to Purbrook? And I want to be called Stella, not Joyce.' My parents consulted Dr Dewhurst, and he advised them it was in my best interests, psychologically, to accede to my requests. Mr Stedman, Headmaster of Purbrook, and Councillor Privett were invited to a meeting with my parents, Miss Sparrow and Dr Dewhurst. Everyone agreed that I might attend Purbrook for the last six weeks of term, starting the following Monday, but I would not be allowed to wear the school uniform until I was ten years old. Officially I was still allocated to Bedhampton.

At the age of ten years I was allowed to enter Purbrook Park County High School officially. The school day started with assembly in the hall. The youngest boys and girls were the first to enter, from opposite sides, and were to line up on two markers, leaving a gap down the centre. Miss Lawson was agitated because none of the girls in my class were willing to lead and this was holding up the rest of the school. I had no qualms at being first into the hall and got annoyed at their reticence, so I calmly strode in front and said 'Follow me!' Lining up on the marker I looked up to see Mr Stedman smiling down at me from the reading desk in front of the stage, approving of my action. So began my years at Purbrook.

The school bus collected pupils from as far away as Emsworth, the furthest point from the school. The final stop was at Bedhampton where, being the last one to board, I had to sit on a box next to the driver, there being no other seat. This 'privilege' enabled the elderly driver the opportunity to give me an occasional treat – an apple from his garden, big and juicy. This fatherly gesture was never forgotten.

That autumn we collected sweet chestnuts from the shrubbery, and Miss Lawson allowed us to cook them on the hot plate of the stove. I think this room must have been the day nursery of the Georgian house. Many times I collected pocketfuls of beech nuts, which were fiddly to open but delicious to eat.

School events such as the choir festival and sports day took place in Winchester annually. For several years our choir entered, and often came second in the county. Every summer the school would travel in several coaches to the annual sports day. This was held in grounds to the south of the town. It was a packed and exciting day. A running track was laid down, and each school was assigned to one section of the grounds. All the schools competed in athletics and cups for the winners were presented at the end of the day. Pupils had to wear uniform and carry packed lunch, but each school was allocated one of the cottages alongside the road for use of their toilets, and lines of pupils formed at their gates. The trek through the cottage gave one an insight into people's living rooms on the way through to the outside loo down the yard.

From an early age Mother encouraged handmade Christmas presents for the family as these would be less costly. I learnt to knit scarves, pullovers, embroidered needle cases in felt, and crochet mats. Cards of buttons and bookmarkers were decorated in script writing for birthdays.

At infant school we were taught plain knitting and we made dishcloths. In the junior school we had to sew by hand the obligatory pinafore. This took a long time and was boring, so when at senior school we progressed to items of underwear and then to summer dresses I was delighted. As I was already adept at hand sewing and using a sewing machine, these were quickly completed.

I vividly remember in 1930 helping Father to reupholster our settee and two chairs. He showed me what he called 'a trick of the trade'. He took a strip of cardboard and deftly hammered tacks through the card and cloth at the top edge of the back. The material was then pulled over and tacked underneath the bottom rail. Using a special needle and thread I was given the job of sewing both sides and this gave a tight finish to the back area. Now I was given the job of pleating and sewing the roundels on the front of the arms. His teaching of the skill of upholstery was never forgotten.

At Purbrook in our art classes we explored many different styles. Exercises in designing repeat patterns were a favourite, especially when allied to a practical application, for example pelmets, cushions, wallpaper or endpapers for books.

Metalwork also intrigued me, and in my last year at Purbrook, we were asked to design something to be made in metal. I decided to draw a panel which could be used as a wall grill or a grill in the pavement. My design incorporated all the skills required by engineering principles. I can only think it was through my father that I aquired these skills at such a young age. Sometimes I found my designs could be transposed into projects in needlework and embroidery.

In 1937 Father started to take an interest in my artwork, and it was then I found him as a friend. To develop my talent he gave me his prize book, *Nature in Ornament*, which influenced my schoolwork to a considerable degree. At the same time he gave me a book called *The Art of Illuminating as Practised in Europe from the Earliest Times* by W. R. Tymms and M. D. Wyatt, architect, the second edition in Octavo published in December 1859. It had originally belonged to my maternal grandfather, who purchased it some time before 1866.

Then I discovered a talent for design following the art nouveau trend of simplistic flowing format. Needing a pair of slippers, I designed a peacock's head in green silk lined with peach. Using different stitches I embroidered and outlined the quilted peacock, extending the wings to form the sides. I attached the fabric to the flanges of a pair of soles and these made warm and comfortable slippers that were worn for many years.

During my last two years at Purbrook the art mistress allowed me, after completing whatever was on the curriculum, to sew and embroider my own projects. One afternoon, having finished my prep and being anxious to finish stitching a cushion cover as a present for Mother, I was quietly working away when the Headmistress, Miss Fountaine, who was taking the homework class, appeared at my side. She enquired in a whisper, 'What are you doing?' Explaining my wish to use every available minute to finish it before the end of term, I showed her what was involved. It was a Spanish design of brilliant colours, worked in wool and gold silk cross-stitch. It was part of the collection of embroideries and silks left to Father by a previous art mistress of the college. One quarter had been completed and the rest was a blank canvas. No chart or pattern was supplied. One had to count every stitch and transpose them in reverse on each of the remaining quarters to complete the cushion. She was most surprised at the intricate detail and amazed at the degree of concentration and skill required. She urged me to be sure to show it to the art mistress at my next class.

2

OUTBREAK OF WAR

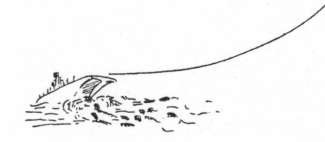

In 1938 we went on a school trip to Dinard, Brittany. Excited at the prospect of my first visit abroad, and to be travelling with my school instead of members of my family, I looked forward to it with great anticipation. As I was the youngest pupil in the group, Mother made one condition. She arranged for me to share a bedroom with an older girl.

We left school in a coach and at Portsmouth harbour boarded the ship for the port of St Malo. The day was sunny, the sea was smooth and I enjoyed the trip. From St Malo we travelled in another coach to our hotel in Dinard, a seaside town. Apparently we were late in arriving, so the teacher who was allocating the bedrooms was under pressure to be quick as the hotel staff were waiting to serve our meal. The girl Mother had asked to look after me decided to room with another, which left me at the end with the last single room! I must admit I felt left out, but was determined to make the best of it. Consequently, until I decided to go off on my own, I was thrown into the company of two boy classmates for most of the time, there being no other girl of my age.

At the supper table we were served with a cup of tea and a slice of a large omelette. We had only had sandwiches for lunch on board ship, and we were all very hungry. Eventually some slices of bread and butter appeared, and I managed to get two slices. Breakfast I knew would be the French croissant and jam – not really enough for my appetite, and lunch seemed a long time coming, but the following supper was more substantial.

One day we made a coach trip to a market where we watched Breton ladies making lace. Being careful of the little pocket money I had, I bought a small lace butterfly and a very small bottle of Chanel No. 5 perfume as a present for Mother. Another day we had a coach trip to Dinan. There, everyone went to the shops to buy cakes and mementoes. Seeing a guide collecting a group of French and German people to be guided around the local castle, I joined them. I was most interested to see the strength of the castle's defences and surprised at the thickness of the walls, although I only partly understood the guide's graphic descriptions of the interesting features as I was not very proficient in the French language at that time.

Our return journey was overnight, and because of fog we had to anchor in the middle of the Channel for several hours. Many people felt seasick with the rolling at anchor but I loved it! That night I developed neuralgia due to a bad tooth and the Headmistress allowed me to sleep on a bench in the open air tucked up with a blanket, as I found the heat in the saloon made it worse. We eventually disembarked at Portsmouth at about 6 a.m. and were taken to a café, where we were given a large English breakfast, appreciated by everyone.

On arriving home I found my cat, Jinky, sitting on the gatepost waiting for me. Mother said he had been pining for me while I was away, but half an hour before I arrived had got up from his basket and gone outside and down the drive to sit on the gatepost. This had always been his favourite place to wait to greet me when I was due home from school. How did he know I was on my way home just half an hour before I arrived? Animal instinct is incredible.

In 1939 I travelled with Maud, another schoolgirl, on an exchange visit to Paris. I was met by Nicole Chabanel and her mother at the Gare du Nord. They lived in an apartment on the Left Bank. I was to stay until 2 September, when Nicole would accompany me back to England for a month.

During the first two weeks we visited the Louvre Museum, where I was impressed with the vigour of the *Winged Victory*. I thought the *Venus de Milo* was very dark and was surprised to find it not as large as pictures had indicated. Other visits were to the tomb of Napoleon and the Notre Dame. My memory of the Sacré Coeur is of a very long flight of steps leading up to the entrance. From there the agrandissement of Montmartre appeared as an interesting collection of small jumbled buildings nestling under the shadow of this famous church.

Another memorable visit was to the Palace of Versailles. The circular bedroom of Marie Antoinette, with its mirrored walls, gilded pillars and blue ceiling dotted with stars, was fantastic. Such a contrast to the almost bare bedroom of King Louis. The long gallery with its fabulous mirrors was very impressive. There were eleven octagonal lampshades in the main gallery and entrance hall and I was told the twelfth hung in the staircase hall of the Petit Maison, the little house that had been built in the garden for Marie Antoinette's amusement.

During my visit Maud and her French exchange girl invited us to tea. When we arrived we were ushered into the best room, where the table was laid with cups and saucers, a jug of milk, a sugar bowl and a plate of biscuits. Two other French girls were introduced and we all sat down. It was obviously an occasion, for the teapot was brought in and ceremoniously placed in the centre of the table. The tea, when served, looked very weak, but this did not bother me. What did was the fact it was COLD!! Among embarrassed giggles, it transpired that the tea had been made with cold water. What could I do but offer to show them how to make 'English Tea'.

During my third week there was a sense of urgency as troops began arriving by road and rail every day. The Tuilerie Gardens became a massive camp with tents everywhere.

Listening to the early morning overseas radio on Thursday 24 August we heard someone recommending all Americans to leave Europe immediately. Turning to Nicole, I said, 'If it's good enough for them, Maud and I should get back to England this weekend, as it appears the outbreak of war is imminent.'

By lunchtime we had contacted Maud and agreed to leave Paris as quickly as possible. Our tickets were checked, and we were told to travel to Calais, where ferries were sailing to Dover continuously. Pooling our money, we went to the post office and sent a cablegram to my father, saying as we were leaving Paris on the midday train would he meet us off the ferry at Dover on Saturday at about 4 p.m.

To my amazement, when arriving at the Gare du Nord, I found not only Maud but also her French exchange girl. Her parents were quite insistent that she was to travel with us, otherwise she would not be able to have her month's holiday in England. So we were bundled on to the train, luckily securing seats, and arrived at Calais about 2 p.m. Following the crowds to the quays, we were shepherded, four-abreast, into a queue which went to and fro in an 'S' formation.

At first we could not see the ferries or even the end of the queue for the hundreds of people with luggage. Moving slowly, snake-wise, we saw one ferry pulling away from the distant quay and within a matter of minutes another one appeared alongside and the queue started to move again. We saw at least five ferries pull in and depart fully loaded before we got within distance of seeing one of the gangways. When we were within the last thirty people from the nearest gangway – off went the ferry to our left. On our right another one was nearing the quay and yet another was steaming along about 6 miles out. At last we got on board and eventually landed at Dover harbour about 7 p.m.

Maud and I were through customs quickly and we waited for her girlfriend, who, being French, had, of course, to go through the foreign side. As she did not appear after ten minutes I left my case with Maud and went through to the other side. No other foreigner was there, and I found this thirteen-year-old girl, with limited English, being questioned by three customs officials. I had to explain what had happened and reassure the immigration officer that she was on a school exchange visit. After giving them the name and address of Maud's parents and accepting the fact that she might have to go back to France, I was allowed to bring her with me. Her suitcase had been taken on to London and it was several days before it arrived back at Havant.

Now where was Father? And the car? After looking around the area where cars were parked for a while, Father suddenly appeared! He said he, Mother, my sister and Maud's mother had watched the arrival of all the ferries from Calais since early afternoon. They were so relieved to see us safe and sound but oh dear – what about the seating in the car? There were too many of us with the luggage! After some discussion I suggested that Maud and I take the train to Havant and we could catch a bus or walk the short distance home. Then there would be room for everyone and our luggage in the car.

At first Mother was very apprehensive about us going all that way by ourselves, but I said if we could arrange to travel from Paris through all the hassle of troop movements in a foreign country, we could surely manage a train journey from Dover to Havant. In the end this was what was decided. Father gave me some money and we walked to the station and bought our tickets. At that time in the evening we had to change at Brighton with an hour's delay.

On this train we were joined by another French girl, who was much older. She was travelling to stay with relatives at 'Ov'. She had booked to Brighton but did not know what to do when she got there! Although her English was good she found it difficult to communicate. At Brighton we offered to help her find the bus. Before leaving the station we made sure of our return to catch the connection to Havant. The man on the gate was very helpful and told us where to catch the bus. There it was to discover buses had stopped running earlier in the evening. As it was now late and she was very tired, I suggested she stay at one of the numerous bed-and-breakfast houses overnight and continue her journey in the morning. Selecting one that proved to be clean and comfortable at five shillings per night, we left her with a pleasant landlady who undertook to see her on the bus for Hove the next morning.

At Havant we were very glad to see Father waiting to take us home. He had been able to take Maud's mother and the French girl to their house in Lower Lane and then leave my sister and Mother at our house with plenty of time to collect us. What a day!

It was not until the following Sunday that a broadcast by Prime Minister Neville Chamberlain was expected. Mother and I joined Father in the drawing room instead of going to church. At 11 o'clock he announced in a sombre tone that a state of war now existed between Germany and Britain. Father turned off the radio and there were a few moments of quiet thought until he turned to Mother and said, 'We must plan for twenty-five years ahead. Examination results must be downgraded immediately otherwise there will be insufficient qualified teachers available for when the war is over. You must stock up on suitable clothing and shoes for the next five years.' Leaving them to discuss what needed to be done I crept out of the room, feeling very apprehensive of what might happen and a little excited at the prospect of a very different life that might be opening up for me. My entry to the College of Art was but a few days away – would I be able to go?

That night the air-raid sirens went off for the first time. We hurried down into our cellar and sat in deck chairs wrapped in eiderdowns, for it was bitterly cold. How poor our preparations had been. This was soon improved by putting down some carpet, and installing better chairs and camping facilities to make a hot drink. We each had a small suitcase to hold emergency clothing and any precious items. At night, even if the mobile guns were firing and travelling up and down the back road, we found we could sleep, as the sound was muted through the ground. My cat soon made himself snug in his bed under a shelf in the corner.

As we were only a short distance from the shore, it was important that no chink of light could be seen at night. Father conformed to the blackout regulations by fitting plywood shutters to the inside of windows in the downstairs rooms behind our heavily lined curtains. Upstairs, blackout curtains were hung underneath pelmets, and only 40-watt bulbs were fitted. Many times on hearing raiders approaching before a warning siren went off we would drop everything and run for our cellar. One day when dog-fights were leaving sky trails, Father and I were standing in our front porch when something landed on the tiles with a clink. It was a piece of shrapnel about 4 inches long, with very jagged edges. It was wise to be under shelter when aircraft were overhead.

No one realised how much basic work in mathematics I had missed due to children's illnesses I had during my time at Bedhampton School. Therefore when I was fifteen years old it became obvious I could not hope to gain a pass in mathematics, one of the four subjects necessary to obtain the school certificate. As the cost of both school and college was the same, Father offered me the choice – a year at art college, or a year in form VI. I opted for the former, which actually gave me a far better grounding for my future.

The Southern College of Art had three colleges, in Bournemouth, Portsmouth and Southampton. The Portsmouth College of Art was on the seventh floor of the two-winged building behind the Guildhall. Mr Edward E. Pullee was the Principal, and my father was Vice Principal. The other floors were occupied by the Technical College.

So in September 1939 I started my year at Portsmouth Art College. I would catch the half-hour train to Portsmouth station with Father and we would walk the half-mile to Bedhampton Halt. Some of our fellow travellers had known Father for many years, and one of them made the following comment to me.

'You must find it awkward to have your father as a tutor?'

I replied, 'No, not really. It is a question of discretion. It's like having two sides of a coin. One side is home and the other is college. Father trusts me not to repeat anything overheard at college or at home. He expects me not to embarrass him in either place. It's quite simple.'

The main door into the entrance hall of the two wings of the colleges was approached by a steep flight of steps. The doorkeeper knew the faces of all the students and would nod his acceptance of one's entry, but he was very quick to challenge a stranger. A square stairwell rose seven floors, and between each floor two flights of stairs were on either side of a mezzanine landing.

As a full-time student I attended morning, afternoon and evening sessions all week. Mr Townsend was head of the Architectural Department and gave me – the only girl – instruction in the art of tracing, where the trick was to leave enough Indian ink on the tracing paper so that it could be printed. He also instructed me in draughtsmanship; that was the skill in using T-squares, set squares, and curves for perspective in architecture. He also allowed me to attend his lectures on building construction with slides from all over the world, which I found most interesting. Father taught me perspective, technical drawing, lettering and pottery. Other tutors gave me instruction in millinery, glove-making, couture dressmaking, embroidery and other crafts. A full quota of learning.

At the end of my first term, a fancy-dress Christmas ball was held for both colleges. On that evening I accompanied my parents, and we were met by the Principal dressed as a Chinese mandarin. Very clever makeup, even down to the fingernails!

During lunch breaks, an architectural student and I had been practising the London Tango. When the London Tango music started, only two couples besides ourselves started to dance. After one circuit I noticed they had stopped to watch us. We used the floor like professionals, forming some very intricate steps. He was dressed as a Spaniard and I was dressed in white sprinkled with playing cards, as 'Patience', so our costumes complemented each other in colour. When the music finished we were given an ovation from the 300 people assembled! My parents could not be embarrassed by my expertise, could they?

The end-of-term notices were given to me to produce, showing the various styles that had been learnt each term. In the summer term of 1940 I was asked to paint in Roman lettering of 6 inches in height, on a board some 5 feet by 3 feet, 'Southampton College of Art Portsmouth Centre'. This was to be hung from the banister of the stairwell so that it could be seen from the entrance hall seven floors below, and it was there for many years.

One day in midsummer, having no coat or umbrella, I paused at the entrance to college, realising the downpour was so heavy I would get soaked running to catch my bus and there was no shelter in front of the Guildhall. Dr Peter Hey, one of the technical tutors, suggested I share his umbrella, as he was to catch the same bus. He knew my father and was obviously concerned at my predicament. On attending a meeting of a local archaeological group at a lady member's house some thirty-four years later and 150 miles distant from Portsmouth, to my utter amazement I found out that her husband was Mr Hey. What a coincidence!

*

For the first few months of the war, life went on more or less as usual – until the first bombs fell on Portsmouth. I was glad on that autumn morning of my navy wool cardigan, school issue though it was, for new clothes could not be bought until old ones wore out.

The architectural room took up the whole of one wing of the building. That morning, the swing doors from the main stairwell gently thudded to behind my desk, and a freckled face appeared over my board. 'You're late,' I said. 'Bus was late!' came the reply. From the far end of the room the master's voice boomed, 'And what time do you call this young man? Hurry up and join us. You'll have to make up for lost time.' A grudging whisper followed; 'Not my fault the bus didn't run is it? Blame the war.' At the end of his lecture Mr Townsend retired to his office, and quiet once more descended on the Drawing Office.

Above our heads the rising wail of the air-raid warning siren started. Mr Townsend emerged, shouting 'Everyone out! Hurry up! This way!', holding open the small door to the spiral staircase that led down to the next level and the concrete stairs to the basement. Leaping off my stool, I grabbed my instrument box and handbag and jumped for the gangway. Seeing the master urging his students through the narrow doorway, it was obvious to us at the other end that it was touch and go whether everyone would get down in the allotted time, let alone us in the rear.

Noting their slow progress, I gasped, 'No way!' and Jenkins, the erstwhile latecomer, made a snap decision, calling out, 'We'll take the main stairs Sir,' and to me he said, 'It'll be quicker. Come on. Run!' We flew hell for leather. Speed was essential and he took the stairs two at a time, urging me to keep up, for we had seven double flights to go. My feet seemed to skim each step with the merest touch, and the aircraft sounds thrumming the air lent extra impetus to our flight.

Running into the basement tunnel, we collided with the senior technical students. A few minutes later we heard Mr Townsend's voice calling, 'Jenkins, are you there?'

'Yes, Sir. Here, Sir.'

'Where is Stella? Is she with you?'

'I'm here,' I managed to splutter, being partially crushed behind a large, hefty engineering student. Thrusting the student aside, Mr Townsend towered above me.

'Thank God you're safe. You must have flown down those stairs.'

Jenkins explained. 'We couldn't have made the spiral stairs, Sir. We didn't have time. We just ran.'

I added, 'Yes, Mr Townsend, we knew we could make it. We're both fast runners.'

He was so relieved and had to agree our sudden action had been for the best. It had been a sensible decision, for we had arrived in the basement before him and the other students! Marking us off his register, all his students now safely accounted for, he smiled benignly and said, 'Join me at the other end when you've got your breath back,' then disappeared.

Panting for breath and shaking from our exertions, we lent against the green-tiled wall. This gave us a sense of security, even though it felt chillingly cold. Suddenly, the wall appeared to shudder and move. We looked at each other aghast. There was no noise.

'Did you feel that?' I asked.

'Yes. What was it?'

'Bombs I expect.'

All that could be heard was the muted throbbing of aircraft penetrating our underground refuge. Had the bombs been aimed at the Guildhall, they could easily have missed and struck the building above us. Gradually the sounds faded away, and the all clear rang out.

Back upstairs we discovered that nobody else had felt the walls move. Incredible, but true. This was the first air raid on Portsmouth when bombs were dropped at North End.

Soon afterwards, on 5 December 1940, a bomb demolished the Carlton cinema in Cosham. Roy S. Pearce, one of my classmates from Purbrook, was killed.

*

Operation Dynamo took place from the end of May to early June 1940. Of the 330,000 men who were rescued from Dunkirk, those who were fit were stationed within 2 miles of the South Coast, ready to repel the impending invasion. Several hundred were under canvas, or quartered in commandeered houses such as Leigh Park House and its grounds just north of Havant. They were allowed out of camp in the evenings for a few hours. Walking down North Street, they would queue two abreast along the pavement for the NAAFI canteen opposite the Congregational church. As they could not cope with the numbers of troops, Mother organised the opening of our church hall in Elm Lane as an additional facility. Ladies attending our church and others from the Church of England volunteered to man this canteen. Extra rations were allocated for this purpose – of tea, sugar, bread, butter, flour and lard.

Our canteen opened at 6 p.m. and closed at 10 p.m. every evening except Sunday. During these hours the ladies worked in relays serving tea, and kept the kitchen ticking over with preparation of food and washing up. A cup of tea cost a ha'penny, a slice of bread and butter was one penny. The crusts were spread with jam, donated from private homes, and cost a ha'penny – these were a great favourite as the troops had very little money. A variety of cakes were made by the ladies at home from the extra supplies. Mother cut the cakes into portions, each costing one penny. If a cake could be evenly portioned, e.g. into six or eight pieces, this was fine. I was roped in to deal with the odd sizes – five, seven or nine portions.

At home we had lots of apples from the allotment, so Mother bought several baking trays, each of four pans. In our kitchen she prepared large basins of sliced apples under water. Another basin held a dry mixture of flour and fat, ready for pastry. With the supplies of flour, fat and a little sugar, she baked apple pies.

One exceptional Friday she cooked some thirty-six pies during the day to take down to the canteen. They cost tuppence each, and were much sought after. When I got home from work soon after 5 p.m., it was to find one batch of twelve in the oven, nearly ready. I prepared another set of three trays while eating my own tea. Then, leaving my batch cooking in the oven, I cycled to the hall and delivered the cooked ones to the kitchen. Back home again, we continued in the same sequence all evening, and by half past nine we had produced over 100 pies. That evening it was calculated that just over 700 cups of tea had been served!

During that evening, having delivered my first batch of pies, a soldier in the queue called out to enquire if, when he got inside, there were going to be any. Estimating the numbers in front of him and the time it would take me to get home and back again I reckoned he would have a good chance. When I returned with the next batch it was to see him just within steps of the table, so I think he got his apple pie.

Visiting Havant in 1993, I walked up North Street to find that little had changed. I made contact with a member of the Congregational church. She sent me a copy of a page from the Havant Congregational Recipe Book that had been produced in June 1924. Both Mrs McIlroy and my mother, Mrs Broughton, had donated their recipes for gingerbread. It reminded me of finding this book inside Mother's big black recipe book when I had started to learn cooking. Mother told me that in 1930, she had considered including her recipe for parkin, at which she was an expert, but considered it not suitable, its being a Yorkshire delicacy. The book was prefaced with the following:

We may live without friends, we may live without books,
But civilised man cannot live without cooks.

As Ruskin was a favourite author of my mother, I believe she was responsible for the inclusion of a quotation from him shown on the leading page.

The original NAAFI building opposite the Congregational church had been built well up off the ground and set back from the road. The metal roof construction can still be viewed inside the present-day pet shop Pampurred Pets, previously Connells Cycle and Toy Centre.

After some months, when Eagle Day had passed and the threat of invasion was over, troops were dispersed to other camps around the country. Our church canteen was no longer required, and the Navy took over Leigh Park and the estate, which then became HMS *Dryad*, the mining department of Portsmouth Dockyard.

*

It was a very hot Wednesday afternoon in 1940 when Mother and I went to visit her friends William and Valletta Slatter in Emsworth. Mr Slatter was a chemist, and had a pharmacy in the High Street. Wednesday was his half-day closing, so we were able to go out for a walk. Crossing the High Street we turned down Nile Street, which ran down to the water. On our right were the ruins of some cottages. These had been bombed a few days before, at the same time as the raid on Portsmouth when I had sheltered in the college basement.

There was a light breeze and it blew something into my eye. Mr Slatter whipped out his eyeglass, turned back my eyelid and with the corner of a pristine white handkerchief removed a minute glass splinter! It was very painful, so we returned to his shop, where he washed out my eye. As the pain persisted, he put in some eye drops which froze the eyeball. That evening my doctor confirmed that the glass splinter had scratched the eyeball and I had to keep it frozen until it healed.

Shortly after our visit, the couple received the devastating news that their only son, Pilot Officer Dudley Malins Slatter, had been shot down over the Channel – 4 miles from Dover. His squadron had only just arrived at Hawkinge and were ordered to patrol 20 miles south of Folkestone. He was a gunner with Pilot Officer J. R. Gardiner in L7016, one of the nine Defiants which had taken off. The squadron had suddenly been attacked by Bf 109s both from above and below them, and within seconds the squadron was decimated. Four were shot down in flames, and Gardiner was the only pilot who was rescued, wounded, from the sea.

The book *Battle of Britain* by Francis K. Mason gives a very descriptive and comprehensive account of this combat. Dudley's body was never recovered, and his name is recorded on Panel ten of the Runnymede Memorial.

Mr and Mrs Slatter were understandably shattered, and wanted a memorial of their own. They asked me to write the details of his life in script under a photograph, and this was framed and hung on their living room wall.

*

Prior to the expected German invasion, code-named 'Sealion', German aircraft made sporadic sorties across the Channel to photograph ports, aerodromes and defences along the South

Coast. The normal procedure was to fly at low level along the Channel, then turn inland for a short distance and fly in a half-circle to head back to France. Consequently, people who lived within 2 miles of the coast did not rely on air-raid sirens as they were unable to give enough warning. We relied upon our ears, listening for changes in the note of an engine to sense the direction any aircraft was taking. This would alert us to take shelter, as German pilots had a tendency to fire at anything that moved. This could be difficult when houses were set back from the road, but was much easier in the country, where hedges, trees and ditches offered instant cover.

During this time there were many occasions when one had to move very swiftly to get out of sight. I recall, for instance, on cycling home to lunch one day, having to throw my bicycle down and run some 10 feet to seek shelter beneath a hedge. At the same time an Austin Seven was abandoned by its driver, who leapt over a wooden fence on the opposite side of the road. It was fortunate that the belt of trees along this fence were very tall, forcing the pilot to climb steeply to avoid crashing into them. As the aircraft circled out to sea I picked up my bicycle and the driver got into his car and drove off, all as a matter of course – we'd been delayed no more than three minutes.

The half-acre of land that Father rented as an allotment lay above and behind the gardens of the houses along the main road. As it was 60 feet above the back road, it was virtually inaccessible. Our only access was made possible by the goodwill of our neighbours, who allowed us to cross their backyards.

It was on open ground so, as a safety measure, we planted rows of runner beans on tripod stakes at right angles to the line of attack by raiders – from east to west – instead of to the southern aspect as was the norm. This proved to be a valuable precaution. One day when I was picking runner beans for lunch, a German aircraft came flying in directly towards our allotment from the south. Throwing myself full length between the rows of stakes and wearing green overalls, I thought it unlikely I could be seen, and the aircraft passed overhead having missed me completely.

Another time when I was digging I heard an aircraft approaching and decided to run for the house. As I ran past the large walnut tree at the corner of our neighbour's garden in order to cross the drive, I saw the aircraft only a few feet above the house, coming directly towards me down the drive. Leaping back, I pressed against the massive tree trunk, thinking bullets could not possibly penetrate. Then realised I would be exposed to the rear gunner as it flew past. So as it went overhead I followed underneath to place myself out of sight against our garage. When I got into our house it was to see Mother in a state of shock, for she had watched the whole incident and feared I had been killed.

A week or so later, Mother's friend and her neighbour were sitting on a settee in the bay window of her bungalow drinking coffee. Hearing a low-flying aircraft approaching, they dropped their mugs and flew out of the room, across the kitchen and into the Anderson shelter by the back door. On their return they found their mugs quite untouched, but there was a line of bullet holes across the settee.

3

HMS *EXCELLENT*

Now these are the Laws of the Navy
Unwritten and varied they be,
And he that is wise will observe them,
Going down in his ship to the sea;
As naught may outrun the destroyer,
Even so with the law and its grip,
For the strength of the ship is the Service
And the strength of the Service, the ship.

Rear Admiral Ronald A. Hopwood, 1896

On leaving college I took a job as a clerk/storekeeper to earn some money – fifteen shillings a week – while I searched for a position in a drawing office. The local firm in Bedhampton had a workshop behind Woolworth's in Havant. There, they repaired engine nacelles, and they needed someone to dispense the stores and deal with the paperwork. After a few months I read a newspaper advertisement inviting applications from tracers to join the experimental Drawing Office of HMS *Excellent* on Whale Island. This was my opportunity.

At the interview I was surprised to see there were twenty-two applicants, all much older than myself. Everyone was given a simple tracing as a test piece of our ability, and when these were collected the result, we were informed, would be decided within a week. Having brought samples of my college work, I approached the Chief Draughtsman and asked if he would like to see them. Looking through my portfolio of drawings, he asked me to wait and left the room. On his return he was very affable, and asked how I intended to get to the office by 8 a.m., as my home was 7 miles away. Although there was a bus route to the end of Stanley Street, I explained it was my intention to cycle all the way on to Whale Island. To my delight, a couple of days later I received a letter appointing me to the job.

My first day at HMS *Excellent* in March 1941 started with a 7-mile cycle ride from Bedhampton, passing through Cosham and over the bridge on to the Portsmouth Island. When I reached Stanley Street, I turned right, down to Whale Island. At the guard hut I was checked, and then directed to follow the road past the parade ground in front of the station house, to park my bicycle under the overhang leading to the Drawing Office above.

The Chief Draughtsman met me and introduced three draughtsmen and Vinny, who was an elderly lady tracer. I discovered later that the name Vinny was related to vinegar. She had a pretty sharp tongue.

My job was basically tracing, but over the next eighteen months I learnt a lot about engineering from those drawings as well as improving my tracing expertise.

One draughtsman was Donald Fry. He lived in Drayton and also cycled. It became the usual thing for us to cycle together at the end of the day. One day, on leaving work at 4 p.m., we fell in with some groups of men from the dockyard who were also cycling homewards – four abreast and slow. As no traffic was coming towards us we drew out and quickly overtook all of them. Quite a feat!

One day in winter there had been a sharp frost. On entering Whale Island I had not realised that the road sloping down from the entrance had experienced the full force of the weather. As I turned to the right my cycle slid from under me – it was sheet ice! Why hadn't the guards warned me? I had to walk some yards before being able to ride again.

Cycling fast one morning, having been held up by traffic, I was nearly halfway past the quarterdeck when 'Taps' was sounded. A Naval sub lieutenant stopped dead in front of me and, turning to face the flag, came to attention. Being so close, I had to jump off my bike very quickly and, being a civilian, I stood still by his side as a matter of courtesy. Out of the corner of his mouth he whispered, 'I thought I could just make it to my quarters.' When 'Taps' was over, he turned and apologised for causing me to crash-stop, and we walked the rest of the way to the corner together, where we parted, me to my office and he to his quarters. Years afterwards when I saw the film *Genevieve*, I was puzzled as to why Kenneth More's face seemed to be so familiar. On reading his book *More or Less* and checking the relevant dates, I realised the sub lieutenant mentioned above was him. No wonder his face was known to me.

Early one Monday morning the Chief Draughtsman was called out to draw up a design for protection shields for the 4 inch gun turrets on board a cruiser which was anchored in the harbour just behind the quarterdeck of HMS *Excellent*. On his return to our office, he quickly sketched the drawings and came over to my desk. He said, 'Clear your board. This is most urgent. These have to be made before the end of the week and it is the first ship to have them fitted.'

Drawings had to be transferred on to linen for permanent record and for printing. As these shields had unusual curvatures, I never forgot them. The minute they were completed he hurried off to start making them – that same day! Many times in my life after leaving this office I have wished I knew the name of that cruiser. Imagine my excitement when, some sixty years later, I glanced across the River Thames to where HMS *Belfast* was anchored and, to my amazement, recognised the curved shields around her 4-inch gun turrets. Any passing pedestrian would have thought me mad as I exclaimed 'That's it!' What a thrill!

Fired with this knowledge, I got in touch with Nick Hewitt, the Exhibition Officer, who, on hearing my story, invited me to visit for a closer look and a chat about the wartime history of the ship.

On close inspection of the fixings and curvature of these protection shields, I was able to confirm my memory of the design.

HMS *Belfast* was commissioned with the Royal Navy on 5 August 1939, and from September operated from Scapa Flow. When leaving the Firth of Forth on 21 November, she sustained major damage on contact with a magnetic mine, and consequently was put out of service and taken down to Devonport for repairs. These took a very long time, during which she was sent to Portsmouth to have her guns checked and made ready for action, and that was when she was anchored off Whale Island. After many years of service, she came to London to rest in the River Thames as a permanent exhibition, being one of the few ships to have survived the war. The Imperial War Museum, of which she is now a part, has issued a comprehensive booklet giving a full account of her meritorious service.

Her sister ship, HMS *Edinburgh*, was on her way back from Murmansk when she was attacked on 30 April 1942 – she sank two days later. On board, her cargo had consisted of some 5 tons of gold bullion, and forty years later, in 1981, these gold bars were recovered.

*

In September 1941 Portsmouth was experiencing many bombing attacks, and it was decided to evacuate the experimental Drawing Office and some civilian clerks to the country. The Navy had commandeered Bordean House, a few miles west of Petersfield. Free transport was provided by a coach, which left Portsmouth at 7 a.m. As Don Fry, who was also a member of my Drawing Office, and I both lived some miles from the rendezvous, it was decided they would pick us up at The George on top of Portsdown Hill every morning. In order for this to happen I would leave home by 6.40 a.m. and cycle to Drayton, where I could park my bicycle in Don's garage, and together we would climb Portsdown to reach The George by 7.30 a.m. We arrived in Petersfield at 9 a.m. There we were allowed a stop of fifteen minutes in order to do some shopping. Then the coach travelled along the valley through the village of Langrish, climbed the hill and turned sharply at the top into the driveway of Bordean House.

Bordean House was a large country mansion set high on a ridge of dense woodland. It had been commandeered by the Navy, and it housed not only the offices from Whale Island, but all the civilian personnel employed there. The library was taken over by the senior Navy officers, the main drawing room was our drawing office and the typists were upstairs in the main bedrooms. It was a large manor house with many cellars and large kitchens. The house was occupied by Navy personnel and the civilian staff were transported every day from Portsmouth to Bordean.

As this was a Naval establishment, the civilian personnel were required to have separate cooking and dining facilities. The Navy had their own quarters, and a small room upstairs was allocated as a kitchen for the civilians. A lady from the village of Langrish came up to the house every day to make the lunch for the civilians. She had a Calor gas unit as an oven and made very good meals on it. One room upstairs near the kitchen was the dining room for the females, and another, smaller, room was for the males. After our lunch all the females – clerks, etc. – had their free time organised for them by the senior clerk. I was not going to be told what to do with my free time – no way. I joined my male colleagues and in the autumn went out with Don and another to pick blackberries from the bushes around the grounds just outside the formal gardens. These blackberries were given to our cook, who made some excellent puddings.

One winter's morning when I set out at half-past seven there had been a heavy fall of snow on top of ice and it was very cold. I was glad to be wearing my navy velour coat and trousers. I left my bicycle in Don's garage and we set out. We walked past the last house, skirted the edge of a small quarry and climbed, keeping an ear on the sound of an aircraft in the distance.

The early morning mist had cleared the top of the hill, but as we neared the gap we heard the engine note change. Scanning the sky over Portsmouth Island, we found everywhere was completely shrouded in dense mist. Desperately searching for a glimpse of this aircraft, we were appalled to see a Junkers 88 emerge, barely half a mile away above the airport, literally at a level with our eyes. 'Quick! Under the hedge!' I shouted, leaping through the gap to throw myself into the hollow, and a moment later Don fell on top of me. The shadow of the Junkers passed over us, and it cleared the last house on the other side of the road by just a few feet. Firing its machine guns, it disappeared out of sight. Later a couple of sheep were found dead. Don scrambled out and turned to help me up. Shaking with shock and spitting out the leaf debris into which my face had been pressed, I spluttered, 'Did you have to fall on top of me?' Smiling with embarrassment, he said, 'Sorry, but there was nowhere else to go.' Of course he was right.

My clothes were covered in mud; thorns and twigs from the hedge cuttings were embedded in my coat. Pulling these out gave us time to get over the shock of the incident. Now it was imperative to move quickly, for we were late. Near the road the last 2 yards of turf were frozen and appeared to be a sheet of thick glass. We had to crawl on hands and knees to get to the surface of the road.

Don raced ahead to the crossroads, and when I caught him up it was to see our coach slowing chugging up from Portsmouth in a line of traffic. On our side the traffic was nose to tail and we could not get across. Frantically jumping up and down, we waved like mad at the driver so that he would wait for us. Then a lorry driver pulled up and signalled us to cross the road in front of him, and thankfully we climbed aboard our coach.

My dishevelled appearance caused the senior girl clerk who was sitting in the front seat to draw her skirt aside with a grimace and a verbal exclamation of disgust. When we joined our colleagues at the rear of the coach they joyfully remarked on the probable activity we had been up to, until we calmly stated we had been dodging a Junkers. Had they not seen it? They had! The driver had stopped halfway up the hill as there was a petrol lorry just in front. If the Junkers had turned towards them, everyone would have had to get out and run like fury. Such were the times we lived in, with no warning sirens, just using our wits to stay alive.

As winter approached, the sailors allowed myself and three colleagues to use their table tennis table, which was in the cellars, for our lunchtime recreation. Two cellars had been made into one space, and the table just fitted between the two projecting support walls. There was only 3 feet on each side and no more than 4 feet at each end. Playing doubles, we became very proficient at scooping shots from the side and lifting drop shots off the ends. Both doorways became crammed with Naval personnel, who applauded our expertise with enthusiasm. I had a great time that winter, in spite of the disapproval of other ladies because I played table tennis with the men. Well, I had to work with them as a colleague and not as a clerk.

During that winter a Naval lieutenant was seen taking advantage of a heavy snowfall to practise his skiing on the slopes of the hill at the rear of the house.

One evening our coach did not arrive. It had broken down, and we were told another mode of transport was on its way. This proved to be a Naval lorry, with a canvas cover and wooden plank seats along both sides. Everyone was helped aboard and an elderly colleague, being a tiny lady, was lifted in by the Chief Petty Officer with ease – such was his strength. He advised all the girls to sit alternately between the men, who linked their arms to prevent us from being thrown about. Tarpaulins were tucked across our knees, and by sitting close together most of us had a reasonable journey in spite of the cold. Some of the girls were too embarrassed to comply with the Chief's advice, and I think they were sorry afterwards. Needless to say the senior clerk (mentioned previously) refused to travel in a lorry, and telephoned home for a car to collect her. With whose petrol ration, we wondered?

4

FROM SHIPS TO SPITFIRES

When I became bored with my job as a tracer in the experimental Drawing Office at Whale Island, Portsmouth. I enquired if there was any way in which I could improve my position, and the reply was, as a girl under twenty-one years and with no HND qualification, there was no possibility of anything else being available. Therefore I decided to look for a more challenging position.

A week later my father, knowing of my wish to obtain a more interesting job, happened to meet Gerald Gingell in the Southern College of Art at Southampton. He was looking for someone who could read plans, elevations and detail drawings, who could draw freehand in perspective, who had perfect lettering and some engineering knowledge and could trace on to linen for the final process before it was printed. Accuracy and secrecy were a priority. He also mentioned no one suitable had come forward, although this job had been advertised throughout the south of England. Did Mr Broughton know of anyone who fulfilled these requirements? Father was delighted to say, 'Yes. I do. My daughter. She is looking for a new job.'

On arriving home, he spoke of this meeting with Gerald Gingell and gave me the telephone number to arrange an interview. The next day I approached the Chief Draughtsman to request permission for time off for the interview. He was very pleased to hear of the proposed job, and told me to use his telephone to contact Supermarine, where it was arranged I would attend on the following Tuesday at 2 p.m. Instructions were given as to location and entry to meet with the Chief Draughtsman, Mr Eric Lovell-Cooper.

On consulting bus and train timetables, it was discovered it would not be possible for me to get to Hursley Park before the time of the interview. This left me with only one alternative – to cycle. The prospect of some 30 odd miles seemed no great hardship, as I had previously undertaken other long journeys. Two days later, the Chief said if Supermarine gave me the job I could leave within the week, as he could find a replacement from the applicants previously interviewed. It seemed to me that someone at Supermarine had been in conversation with him and wheels were set in motion. Was I right?

Tuesday dawned bright and clear and it was a sheer delight to hear my wheels humming merrily as I traversed up and down hills in a westerly direction. Crossing the main road at Eastleigh, I came at last to Hursley village. The entrance to Hursley Park was guarded by a military post and, having shown my pass, I was directed up the drive to another gate just before the main house. Here, having parked my bicycle, I was escorted down some steps into a hangar which was half underground and covered with camouflaged netting.

After a quick wash and brush-up, I was shown into the Chief Draughtsman's office to meet Mr Lovell-Cooper, exactly on time. My first impression was of a very tall, large man with a stern visage and a gruff voice. Quickly noting my name and address, he introduced Gerald Gingell, section leader of Technical Publications. I stated that I could not speak specifically about my work at HMS *Excellent*, other than to say that the Chief Draughtsman was complimentary of my tracing ability, as I had signed the Official Secrets Act.

Mr Lovell-Cooper then enquired of Mr Gingell if he considered that I was competent to do the job required. His reply was 'Yes, Sir. Absolutely.' The next question was 'When can you start?' My reply was 'Immediately', as there was no problem replacing me in the Whale Island office. In order to arrange accommodation and to have a short holiday, I requested a week's delay.

Lodgings would have to be found in Winchester, as I could not commute from home. This was agreed, and my starting date was confirmed as the following Monday of May 1941. My father suggested I should lodge in the same house as the one in which he had been living for four nights every week, since the evacuation of the Portsmouth College of Art to Winchester. His landlady agreed to this arrangement with a few provisos, mentioned in the next chapter.

The next day I called at the Portsmouth Labour Exchange to transfer my green card work permit from Portsmouth to Winchester. They promised it would be ready for me to collect at the end of the next week. On Tuesday, thinking it might be advisable to check this had been done, I dialled from a telephone box. Somehow I was put directly through to the office in the Labour Exchange that dealt with the movement of labour. Incidentally eavesdropping on a conversation between two officials before I could speak, this is what I heard: 'Oh, very well. We will send out call-up papers for all girls born in 1923 tomorrow.' I replaced the receiver very gently. This was horrendous news! My call-up papers would arrive in the week I was unemployed, before I started employment with Supermarine. There was no way I was going to let this happen and I ran for the bus home.

I was not expected before late afternoon, so Mother was most surprised to see me back before lunch. My explanation, that I had found out I would be called up for the forces if I was not employed before the end of the week, gave her a shock. By that evening I had packed my case and was all set to join Father at his lodgings. Arriving in Winchester in the middle of Wednesday afternoon, I went straight to the Labour Exchange to collect my green card work permit, knowing it was extremely unlikely it would be there. I prepared myself for an almighty bluff if this was so, secure in the knowledge that Lord Beaverbrook had given Supermarine *carte blanche* to employ any person from any occupation or area. It was imperative that I started at Supermarine the next morning.

The Labour Exchange was a small hut with a corrugated iron roof. Inside, a wooden counter stretched across, and two conscripted lady clerks were sitting behind this with a senior woman seated at a desk. At the counter I enquired for my green card, explaining, when she could not find it, that Portsmouth Labour Exchange had promised to send it to them for me to start work at Supermarine.

The senior clerk then came forward and, telling the other clerks to get on with their work, she dictatorially stated I could not decide to move from one job to another, let alone in another area. Jobs had to be advertised, etc., etc., and I was to go back to Portsmouth and take any job in that area. She continued to reprimand me for thinking I could get whatever job I liked, much to the embarrassment of her clerks.

Fuming with anger at such rudeness from her senior position to a young girl, I reacted by striking both hands flat on the wooden counter, and in a very strong but restrained voice loudly stated, 'Did you not know that this post with Supermarine HAS been advertised for the last SIX months throughout the whole of the south of England and no one has been found with all the necessary qualifications? I have been interviewed and chosen to fill this position and I am instructed to start immediately.' As she continued to bluster, I calmly picked up my coat and suitcase and said firmly, 'When my card arrives you will please forward it to Supermarine,' and walked out, shutting the door behind me. Outside, I was surprised at my temerity in speaking as I did to that senior official, but I was determined that nothing and no one was going to stop me.

The next morning I caught the firm's bus and arrived at the gate to the Drawing Office, where one of the guards escorted me to Gerry Gingell's desk. He was amazed to see me, but when he heard what had happened he poured me a cup of tea and sat me down at his desk and told me to wait. He disappeared out of the hangar to see the Employment Manager in the main house. Ten minutes later he returned beaming broadly, 'That's all right. You start today!' I was so relieved that in spite of all the obstacles I had achieved my goal.

Don, having also left HMS *Excellent*, had gone to work at Fort Ridley. Having secured my post with Supermarine, on my way home on Saturday I called at the fort and requested to speak to Don in order to tell him I would no longer be at Whale Island. Of course I was not allowed to enter the fort, but he came out and we had a short conversation. At that time he told me he was also leaving to go to South Africa to work on radar to help our ships in the South Atlantic. Many years later I tried to contact him, but as his wife had died he had gone to live elsewhere. Later I heard he was in a home on Hayling Island, but I heard this too late – he had died.

Top left: 1. Stella Broughton, aged 20, at the party of 3 June 1944.

Top right: 2. Stella Broughton, aged 21, in September 1944.

Right: 3. Charles Henry Broughton, Stella's father and Vice Principal of the Southern College of Art in Portsmouth, photographed in 1937.

4. The Portsmouth Blitz. (*Smitten City: The Story of Portsmouth under Blitz*, *The Evening News*, Portsmouth)

5. Portsmouth Cathedral surrounded by bomb damage. (*Smitten City: The Story of Portsmouth under Blitz*, *The Evening News*, Portsmouth)

6 & 7. Modern photographs of Portsmouth's anti-aircraft defences. (Henry Buckton)

Above: 8.
Hursley Park
House, 1940.

Left: 9.
Jeffrey Quill,
Supermarine's
first Chief Test
Pilot.

10. Joseph Smith, Chief Designer at Supermarine.

11. Alan Clifton, Chief Technician at Supermarine.

12. Photograph of the Supermarine personnel at Hursley Park House. Stella is number 27.

13. Supermarine's Drawing Office. (Solent Sky Museum)

14. Birthday card to Pauline Marren from Drawing Office colleagues in 1945. Drawing by Stella Broughton.

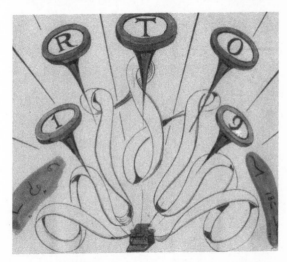

15. Birthday card to Peg Jefferies, typist of Supermarine. Drawing by Stella Broughton.

16. Birthday card to Audrey Tillen, Electrical Section of Supermarine. Drawing by Stella Broughton.

Above: 17. HMS *Belfast*. Drawing by Stella Rutter.

Below left: 18. A metal grill design by Stella at the age of 16 in 1939.

Below right: 19. Christmas card to the drawing office of HMS *Excellent* from Stella Broughton.

Bottom left: 20. Peacock slipper design by Stella, 1939.

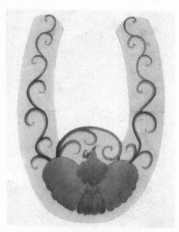

TO THE EXP. DRAWING OFFICE
H. M.S. EXCELLENT.

Merry
Christmas
AND A
Happy
New Year.

STELLA
BROUGHTON
XMAS 1944

21. Stella at the farewell party of 3 June 1944. Drawing by Stella Broughton.

22. The Allied leaders. (J&C McCutcheon Collection)

23. General Eisenhower. (J&C McCutcheon Collection)

24. Field Marshal Montgomery.
(J&C McCutcheon Collection)

25. Omar Bradley. (J&C
McCutcheon Collection)

26. Aircraft waiting to take off before D-Day. (J&C McCutcheon Collection)

27. Pilots on their way to the D-Day landings. (J&C McCutcheon Collection)

28. Part of the airborne armada of 5 June 1944 nearing the French coast. (J&C McCutcheon Collection)

29. Hamilcar gliders landing in Normandy on D-Day. (J&C McCutcheon Collection)

30. Portsmouth dockyard under attack. (*Smitten City: The Story of Portsmouth under Blitz*, *The Evening News*, Portsmouth)

31. Visiting the troops – Winston Churchill prior to D-Day in Hampshire. (Michael Virtue, Virtue Books)

32. Damage in Hampshire after the V1 flying bomb. (*Smitten City: The Story of Portsmouth under Blitz, The Evening News*, Portsmouth)

33. Spitfires of the Sea – Second World War motorboats. (Michael Virtue, Virtue Books)

Above: 34. Supermarine produced other aircraft during the war, including the Walrus (shown here), an air-sea rescue plane. (Michael Virtue, Virtue Books)

Left: 35. A Supermarine advertisement. (Dilip Sarkar)

5

SUPERMARINE

The Unpayable Debt

Willingly they answered the country's call
Gave up their peace time living to fight for us all.
From cities and hamlets, fenlands and hills
From the Empire they came offering their skills.

Ground Staff and Aircrew they each played a part
In taking the war straight to the enemy's heart.
So many died that we might live in peace
That our unpayable debt can only increase.

Some decades later and older than their years
They returned to reflect and share silent tears,
Remembering when conflict filled the sky and earth
And each of them proved to be more than his worth.

The unchanged winding lanes welcomed them back
To the nearby village church and a special plaque
Which in sombre metal on sacred stone
Acknowledges that debt for which we cannot atone.

                                             Joyce Lucas

On my first day at Supermarine I left home about 6 a.m. After having packed my bike with all I needed for the next week, I started to climb up to Portsdown Hill – a climb of six in one! Past Fort Widley turned down Pigeon House Lane. For 3 miles there was no need to pedal. Then on past the villages of Southwick, Wickham, on to East Leigh and through the village to find the main gate of Hursley House. This gate was guarded by military personnel. They checked my pass and directed me to follow the drive. I noted there was a 6-foot-high metal chain fence all along the left side of the drive right up to the house. On the other side there was only grass into the distance. On the left there appeared to be some kind of forest, and there was a close line of trees near the fence.

Hursley House was an eighteenth-century Queen Anne-style mansion. Parking my bike, I entered under a magnificent portico to find a Supermarine guard, who sent me back along the drive to find another gate between the gardens and the line of trees.

There another guard escorted me past the guard hut built under the first tree, down a flight of steps and into the Drawing Office to meet Mr Lovell-Cooper, the Chief Draughtsman – exactly at 2 p.m.

The DO was an aircraft hangar built underground, and was covered with a huge camouflaged net extending from the tree line, across the hangar and far into the grass of the field. It was well concealed from the air.

The Drawing Office comprised some 200 draughtsmen, and my appointment had caused some embarrassment at the fact I would be the first female of under twenty-one years to sit at a board!

As the Technical Publications section under Gerald Gingell was adjacent to the all-female, glass-enclosed tracing office, it was decided to place me on a drawing board there, but next to the glass wall where I could be in touch with Gerry. Everyone thought I was under the head tracer until the Drawing Office was reorganised a year later. The tracers were of different ages, and some were rather dismissive of what they called 'pretty pictures'. The head tracer of course was well aware of my skills, and also the fact that my wages were considerably higher than those under her, who were still in apprenticeship and of the same age. She was to be congratulated on her ability to pass me my pay packet every week without anyone else observing it.

On my first day I was given a huge pile of pencil drawings made by the three artist draughtsmen under Gerald Gingell. It was my job to transfer these drawings on to linen in Indian ink ready for printing. When so doing, I had to clean up any wobbly lines to produce clear drawings and use my lettering skills to clarify the instructions. These perspective drawings had been drawn up by artist draughtsmen with no knowledge of the intricacies of laying ink on to linen. It was up to me to finalise the masters.

In those days females worked as tracers and men were draughtsmen, but I learnt both skills. First, tracers had to learn how to lay Indian ink on to special blue linen for printing purposes. The ink had to be dense – not thin. It could be tricky to have enough ink in your pen so that it did not run out before completing a line. If one made a mistake it could be disastrous. Fortunately I had a very good hard green rubber, which could, with gentle application, erase any mistake. I had learnt to use tee squares at college to create a precise 90-degree angle, and set squares for other angles. In my work for Supermarine, I had to use many other tools, including curves, as the drawings were in perspective.

During the following year I steadily reduced this pile, in spite of additional work being added every day; everyone was racing to get modifications drawn up and out to the production units.

One day some time later, Gerry told me that the drawings I had been given to do were to be sent to North Africa. A motorcyclist was waiting at the gate to get them to London, where they would then be put into the crates and sent to General Montgomery. They would be opened by people who could not understand much English. It was only recently that I heard Spitfire crates had also been sent to Burma to Lord Mountbatten. Should these ever be found, my drawings will be inside to show how to assemble the Spitfire parts!

The hours were from 8.30 a.m. to 5.30 p.m. Monday to Friday, and half a day Saturday till twelve noon. At 11 a.m. each day we were served with a free cup of tea and a biscuit at our desks. Management did not pay for their lunches in the dining room. All staff paid a shilling per day for their lunches. The staff from the house and hutments used the canteen in the basement. The Drawing Office staff were served in their own canteen hut in the grounds. The lunches were well balanced and varied, using meat, cod or herring, or one ounce of cheddar cheese dipped in batter and deep fried, all served with potatoes and a green vegetable. The puddings were often of rice, sago or similar – a portion of sponge, or 'spotted dick', all served with custard. When our timetable changed and we were working until 7 p.m., we were given a 4.30 p.m. tea break of twenty minutes, where a free cup of tea, a sandwich and a piece of cake were served at our desks.

When Lord Beaverbrook requisitioned Hursley House and estate from Lady Cooper, it was agreed she could still occupy the top floor. But shortly afterwards a fire broke out in her rooms, and she was then considered to be too much of a risk for the firm of Supermarine and had to leave.

I did not see inside Hursley House until I became the 'postman' for Gerry. He would often ask me to deliver papers directly into certain people's hands. I would walk through the gardens and enter through the glass portico into the main corridor. The stress office was on the right and the ballroom was on the left (all closed up). I would pass the entrance hall on the right and proceed into the staircase hall. This stairway soared upwards to the attics. Joseph Smith had his office in the library off the space, and a small room connected was Alan Clifton's office. I was never required to enter any of the offices upstairs.

One year it became necessary to cull a twelve-point deer from a herd on the estate. It was a huge animal, and it hung from the ceiling to the floor in the basement corridor of Hursley House for a week. As it was not possible to serve the cooked venison to both canteens at the same time it was arranged for the Drawing Office canteen to be closed that day. All the employees were to take their lunches in the house canteen at different times. It made quite a change, not only in our routine, but in mixing with other departmental people with whom we had little contact.

After lunch at Supermarine all the men would go off, and as I had little in common with any of the female staff I would go back to the DO. There I would sit and spend my lunchtime breaks with original Supermariners such as Reginald Dickson, Gerald Gingell, Alan Clifton or Reg L. Caunter, the head of mods (he took over as Chief Draughtsman when Mr Cooper retired). Jack Rasmussen, the rep from MOD, in his special capacity, was another with whom I spent many a break. We would talk about gardens and growing vegetables, the history of houses, art, museums, etc. Sometimes other senior managers would stroll down from the house to join us. No wonder my face was known.

In summer 1942 we had a visitor, namely Mr H. J. Payn, whose nickname was 'Agony'. He had worked with R. J. Mitchell, but having a German wife had had to leave Supermarine. After calling on Joseph Smith, he came down to talk to Gerry Gingell, who was now in charge of his old section. Afterwards he came to my desk and said, 'Stella, you are doing an excellent job, but did you know that one day saved on your desk is one day saved in getting it to London and is one week in getting it out to its destination?' It was then I realised the importance of speed in my job.

Due to the pressure of the demand for Spitfires and Seafires to aid the war effort, the structure and personnel of the original departments throughout Supermarine had to be increased. In some of the sections, family members of staff were conscripted. This decision aided the security of the work and created a feel of 'family' within the firm. Lord Beaverbrook gave Supermarine *carte blanche* to commandeer anyone who had the necessary expertise to improve the situation. One of my colleagues who had joined the forces was seconded to Supermarine. This was an unusual example, as he wore RAF uniform but was not subject to RAF discipline.

When I joined the Drawing Office I noticed that as a consequence of the influx, members of each section tended to converse and socialise within their own group. Work was rarely discussed, thereby keeping the processes of development on the basis of 'the need to know'.

My first Christmas after leaving Whale Island I sent them a card which showed a Spitfire soaring above a Naval ship to represent my change of occupation. When, many months later, two girls were added to our section, I drew a birthday card for one of them. This depicted the heads of our team carrying tee squares, on which they all wrote their signatures. Later I was asked to design a birthday card for a typist in another department. Their team signed on the ribbon emerging from the typewriter.

*

From a civilian point of view my experience of landladies during wartime was somewhat different to those who were billeted by their departmental officers, such as Irene Young in her book *Enigma Variations*.

When joining Supermarine in May 1942 it was necessary for me to find accommodation close by, as it was impossible to commute daily from home. There was a firm's bus service from Winchester to Hursley Park so it was logical for me stay at the same house as the one my father lodged in during the week. This was quite an experience. The landlady would only take me if I made my own breakfast and sat in the kitchen. Also, before leaving the house I was to take a glass of hot water to her in her bedroom. Having been brought up to cook and housekeep from an early age, this was no problem. She would leave tea, milk, two slices of bread and marmalade on the kitchen table. Sometimes there would be a herring or a kipper, or, as a special treat, an egg!

The evening meal was served in the dining room. Every week it was the same menu. Monday – stew. Tuesday – cold meat and salad. Wednesday – meat pie. Thursday – sausages. Friday – fish.

All meals were served with various vegetables, and followed by a pudding made with milk. Evenings were spent in the drawing room, with Father reading his newspaper and myself occupied with knitting or needlework. Often we played a game of bezique or chess. Rather a dull life, but no more so than was usual at home. When Father decided to semi-retire, thereby only being in Winchester for two nights a week, our landlady informed us that she was going to take a relative to live in as a companion and I had to find other accommodation.

This time it was with a family. The father was employed in the local town council while his wife kept house and looked after their lodgers. Meals were taken at a large table in the downstairs kitchen, and timing was crucial in this household. Breakfast was served on the dot at 7.30 a.m. to their daughter and myself, and half an hour later we were ushered out of the house. Then it was breakfast for the two gentlemen, for they had to leave by 8.30 a.m. At 6 p.m. everyone sat down to the evening meal. As I was under twenty-one years of age, this landlady was inclined to treat me in the same way as her teenage daughter. After dinner we girls were expected to clear the table and wash up the dishes before joining the adults in the lounge, until other duties such as homework or letter writing enabled us to retire to our rooms. Mine was the smallest room, having just a bed, chair and chest of drawers. Sometimes I was able to stay over the weekend, which gave me the opportunity to lunch in town, do some shopping and visit the cathedral. On Sundays at the Congregational church I met up with a group of young people, and we called ourselves the 'Good Companions'. We were all under twenty-one, and we put together a two-hour show of items and a short play to raise funds for the church charities. I missed being in the school choir, and wanted to continue training my voice. I was very fortunate to be able to study under the choirmaster of the cathedral, but as my job became more demanding I had to give up these activities.

One evening at the dinner table I was very embarrassed to be taken to task by the landlady. She wanted to know what I did at work, and with whom? All I could say was that I worked on a drawing board and, having signed the Official Secrets Act, I could not discuss my work. This did not satisfy her, and she continued to ask for answers. Looking to Father for help, I saw that he was astounded at her complete lack of concern regarding security, and could not speak. It was her husband who came to my rescue, telling her in no uncertain terms to stop her questioning and the meal ended in silence. Feeling very shaken and upset by this incident, which appeared to challenge my veracity and showed her indifference to the posters stating 'Careless Talk Costs Lives', I decided to find a more harmonious lodging elsewhere, particularly as Father was to leave Winchester at the end of term.

Fortunately at work I heard that one of the cleaners had a room to let. Within a week I was safely installed at 89 Battery Hill with Mrs Ward, her mother and three boys. She was a widow, dependent upon the income from several part-time jobs, and letting a room was essential. She never alluded to my work or allowed her mother to ask questions, as she had also signed the Official Secrets Act. The fact that she swept the office floor and cleared my wastepaper basket was never mentioned.

Grandma kept house, cooked the meals and supervised the children out of school hours. This enabled Mrs Ward to attend her different jobs. In spite of the strict rationing we were all well fed. Grandma was a dab hand at making scrambled egg from the dried powder, and this was a favourite breakfast dish. Cheap cuts

of meat cooked very slowly with vegetables from the back garden
and potatoes from the market made sustaining meals. These were
followed by puddings, either milk or sponges, baked or steamed
with whatever fruit came to hand, with custard. No cream then – it
was too expensive. In the autumn on Sundays I would often go out
with a packed lunch and come back with pounds of blackberries.
Nothing was ever wasted.

*

One Saturday, not having been home for several weeks, I
was cycling along West Street, Havant, when I became aware
that people were staring at me. As I parked my bicycle on the
forecourt of Woolworth's more people seemed to appear from
nowhere, and congregated in groups, whispering together. What
was going on?

At the counter I asked the young assistant for the items Mother
had asked me to buy, and she promptly dissolved into giggles. At
this, the supervisor stepped forward and took over serving me.
Having paid her, I left the shop, only to discover a crowd had
collected. Quickly getting on my bike I made for home, feeling as
though I had stepped into a weird dimension.

At home I asked Mother what had caused people to turn and
stare at me. Was wearing shorts considered 'fast', or was it because
I was not in any kind of uniform when all my age group were in
one of the forces. Very odd! She was obviously embarrassed by my
questioning, but I pressed her for a reply. Eventually she said, 'Well.
It has been rumoured that Deanna Durbin is staying somewhere
nearby.' I was flabbergasted and could not speak, realising, of
course, that I did look like her.

No wonder my occasional visits home, which varied between two to four weeks on Saturdays, fuelled the rumour.

*

During the war years many stage personalities and musical celebrities gave concerts to people who would not otherwise have had the opportunity to visit theatres or other centres of entertainment. In London musical events were held in the foyer of the National Gallery. This music could be heard by crowds sitting outside in Trafalgar Square. By the same token, factories where conscripted personnel were working for the war effort had visits from various entertainers. At Hursley in 1942 some of these performed in the hut, which was the canteen for the Drawing Office.

In the Winchester Guildhall many other events were held, including the table tennis competitions mentioned elsewhere. The Guildhall was also the venue for dances, with music by the Glen Miller and the Squadronaires. Musical evenings were a great attraction in Winchester and two of these were given by Dame Myra Hess and Benno Moiseiwitsch, both of which I was able to attend. As all transport closed down by 10 p.m., entertainment centres and the cinema had to close early. I became accustomed to walking the 2½ miles back to my digs at Battery Hill in the blackout. One had to rely upon the slight variation of darkness between the houses, skyline and trees if there was no moon. Trailing one's fingers along the walls by the side of the path and the sound of the hedges rustling in the wind would often orientate one.

In 1943, to give a little variance to our concentrated routine, a sports week was planned – the house versus the Drawing Office.

A football match was easy to organise with men. Then someone thought up the idea of a three-legged race of both sexes. Being the only girl in the Drawing Office, I was roped in. At 5 feet 2 inches in height I was teamed up with Noel Mills, who was 6 feet tall! We had only a few minutes to practice but came in a close second. We were very pleased with our result but I am sure if we had been given prior notice and a little more time to adjust, we would have won. Many Supermariners who had joined the Spitfire Society greeted me at our stands at Air Shows. On 12 July 1986 at a Spitfire stand at Middle Wallop one of these was Noel, and he was accompanied by his wife.

Visiting old haunts I met up with Mrs Ward, my wartime landlady, now very elderly. We had a long conversation and she recalled my time with her all those years ago. Her eldest son David had become an expert on helicopters – not surprising when all her lodgers had been involved in the aircraft industry. Finding the address of Mr Eric Lovell-Cooper I took a bus to Golden Common and called upon him, hoping he would be able to recall certain events. At the age of eighty-two he was unable to remember them.

Then, travelling to Hursley and Ampfield, I was able to photograph the site of the 1944 British and American officers' mess hut and the path to Hursley village, which I remember from my visit. The telephone cables that served that camp are still in place.

There were many poems written by people at Hursley, but the one I thought the best was 'Subcontracts' or 'The Mad House' by R. B. Bennett. It shows the frustration of trying to produce the numbers of Spitfires required by the government at the time when our backs were to the wall. Here it is for your perusal:

SUB-CONTRACTS

This is the home of trouble, we get it day and night,
On the carpet, on the 'phone, Sub-Contracts can't be right.
No matter how we struggle with contracts short or long,
We cannot get the bloomin' reqs – and when we do they're wrong.
There are no rivets at the stores, we cannot get the screws,
They change the mod: on every job and then the drawings lose.
It's true that washers can't be spared and bolts just don't exist
While mild steel and alclad sheet are never on the list.
The typists scream, the 'phones go mad, the din is just appalling,
We've been shot down in flames again – without a chance of
stalling.
The shortage list assumes a state of frightening proportions,
Deliveries are down to nil, despite our mad contortions
Production, Spares and the P.R.U, they give us all the shudders,
We can't get struts or Tail Planes, Oleo legs are tricky,
Ribs from Beaton's just as bad, And Wings are awful sticky,
Jettison Tanks and Oil Tanks, we tank they drive us crazy,
We pace the bedroom every night, and come back just as hazy.
Before this war is over, and there ain't no 'Ifs' or 'Buts',
We'll find ourselves in padded cells, completely 'slotted nuts'.
But ere this fate befalls us, we'll prove conclusively,
That Spitfires still command the skies – just you wait and see!

Written by R. B. Bennett, Vickers Supermarine, 1942

*

In early January 1943, the tracing office had to move to another
building to allow the enclosed area in the drawing office to be

allocated to the secret project – Spiteful – under the leadership of Bill Fear. This meant I had to move into the main drawing office. The telephone on Bill Fear's desk was just by the door, and if the door was open – it usually was – the conversation could be heard by whomsoever worked on the first two desks in the main drawing office. Reginald Dickson, who collaborated with Bill Fear in this project, sat at the first desk and, being deaf, would not have heard anything that was said.

As I waited for Gerry, my section leader, to tell me where I was to work, Mr Cooper, the Chief Draughtsman, who was checking all the changes of staff movement, came up to Gerry and asked, 'Are you going to sit behind Dickson?' Gerry's reply astonished me. 'Oh. No. I am going to put Stella there. She can be trusted not to repeat anything she might hear. I will stay at the back.' It was then that I, the first female, was allowed to sit with my colleagues in the main office. It was then I understood my security level in the firm was at a pretty high level.

During the previous year my salary had steadily increased every six months to the extent that it superseded what was considered the norm for my age. While I was still under twenty-one, my salary was increased to £3 per week, the same standard as a draughtsman, which was an unheard-of precedent. I did not realise at the time that my integrity had been so recognised by my superiors. But later this was borne out by the special tasks I was given to do, which were not part of the work of my section. These were given to me directly by Joseph Smith, the Chief Designer.

On one occasion he asked me if I would be willing to make new tracings of several detail drawings that had been done by another office. It was clear to me that whoever had processed them had not laid down sufficient ink to allow them to be printed, and this had caused considerable embarrassment. It only took a couple of days for me to redraw them.

On another occasion I was summoned to Mr Cooper's office, where Joseph Smith proceeded to give me certain instructions. To save time in reproducing a particular drawing, I was to change the title on a master tracing from Spitfire to Spiteful. This name was the top secret of Bill Fear's section, and I was told that Gerry had been instructed not to enquire as to the work I was given! Furthermore, I was to keep my work under cover at all times, and if I wished to leave my desk he was to guard it until my return. This meant we had to split our lunchtimes for the next couple of days. At a later date I had to change another master tracing from Spitfire to Seafang.

The next month Gerry asked me to draw up the control panel of the aircraft that was in the experimental hangar by the Hursley gate. Transport was not required because luckily I had my bicycle. It was quite a distance, passing the house and gardens and cycling down the mile-long drive through the grounds. At the hangar, as I was wearing a skirt, the foreman followed me closely up the steps of the scaffolding and helped me climb in the cockpit. It was not easy to see where to put my feet and there was no seat installed, so he grabbed a parachute pack for me to sit on. A bit uncomfortable, but at least I could see the panel. It was covered in dials of varying sizes and I found it tricky to draw a picture.

At one of the Supermarine reunions held in Southampton, Stanley Seve came up to me and said 'I remember you. You came into the experimental hangar and climbed in the cockpit of the Spiteful. I was one of the fitters and we all wondered who you were and why you were allowed to see the Spiteful when its design was top secret.' At the same reunion I met up with some of Bill Fear's staff, and found that not one of them had any knowledge of my involvement in their work. They were astounded at how well this secret had been kept. Only Joseph Smith, Alan Clifton, Eric Lovell-Cooper and Bill Fear were privy to my participation.

*

Being totally deaf, Reginald Dickson was nicknamed Deafy by all and sundry. There are many unusual stories about him. One person told me that before the war he often saw him cycling to work and reading a book at the same time!

I met Innes Grant at a Supermarine reunion on 16 November 1993, and was reminded by John McDonagh of an incident Innes had experienced with Deafy. He had picked Innes up from work and they were travelling one lunchtime in his car, a Ford 8, to have a drink at a pub called The Clump before going on to Bassett Close East. Suddenly, switching off the engine and flinging open his door, Reginald fled into the ditch on the far side of the road, leaving the car to gently roll forward. Innes, not knowing why he took this action, decided to emulate it on his side, and a few moments later a bomb landed on the road ahead! Dickson's explanation was that he had felt the change in the atmospheric pressure and realised a bomb was descending just above them.

Of course, he could not have heard anything, as he was profoundly deaf. But he had obviously experienced the same pressure on previous raids in Southampton, and had immediately recognised the signs. Had they continued their journey, they would have been killed.

Many pupils in my class at senior school took up the craze of learning the deaf-and-dumb alphabet, at which I had quickly become adept. Deafy Dickson's desk was just in front of mine, and this skill proved extremely useful in January 1943. Joseph Smith, Chief Designer, and Alan Clifton, Chief Technician, accompanied by several visitors, came down to Bill Fear's office for a conference. The test pilots, Jeffrey Quill and Alex Henshaw, were also there. On their way through the Drawing Office they were joined by Eric Lovell-Cooper, Chief Draughtsman, and Jack Rasmussen, the Ministry of Aircraft Production liaison officer. Shortly afterwards they, and others from Bill's section, congregated around Deafy's desk.

Deafy could read lips extremely well and could communicate quite freely with everyone, so I was surprised to see his face appear over the edge of my board and to hear him say, 'Stella, come and tell me what he is saying please, I can't understand him,' indicating one of the visitors from the Ministry of Aircraft Production. I was glad to help, but it was an enormous challenge to deal with not only technical terms but also details on a subject of which I had no knowledge, it being the design and data of the new wing for Spiteful.

Later Bill told me how pleased and intrigued everyone had been at how I was able to keep up with the questions and answers between two and sometimes three people, at a pace that allowed normal conversation to flow. This was mainly, in my opinion, because Deafy could 'read on' words after a few letters coupled with my lips, thus speeding up the process of communication. After this episode I was often called upon to 'talk' with Deafy and his colleagues, as it saved time not having to write details down.

In a letter to me of 1992, Jeffrey Quill wrote, 'Deafy was a remarkable man and his contribution to the success of the Spitfire was very, very great. After the war he went to the USA and became a Technical Vice President of Lockheed.'

My own memory is of a bright cheerful countenance peering over the edge of my drawing board every day. One noticed his great energy and concentration. Time was not wasted in trivialities. The job was to find the solution to problems.

*

At Supermarine we were working the usual eight hours a day and a half day on Saturdays. Every weekend, leaving the office at twelve noon, I cycled some 30-odd miles to arrive home before teatime. As Mother was of advanced years now she relied heavily on me to deal with the household chores of cleaning and washing, as though I was still living at home. After lunch on Sundays I would have to leave by four o'clock to cycle back to my lodgings ready for work on Monday morning. This routine was not only exhausting but did not allow enough time for my own recreation, nor could it be done in the approaching winter. I had to find a solution to this problem.

I went to see Mr Cooper and told him I did not have enough time to assist Mother at the weekends. I suggested that, if I could have a night's rest before cycling to work every Monday morning, thereby losing half an hour's work time, I could make up the lost time by working one Sunday every seven weeks. This was agreed and it worked very well for the next few months.

The timetable change I had adopted appeared to be successful both for myself and the work. Consequently, having noted how well it worked, Eric Cooper probably consulted Joseph Smith about the inability of his men to spend a night at home during the normal weekend. Many company employees came from far afield, necessitating several hours' travel on the railway. Joseph Smith decreed that a different work schedule should now be adopted, especially in expectation of the increased workload. The new schedule comprised twelve ten-hour working days. Two complete days, Saturday and Sunday, were our free time off. This would allow the men to have at least one complete night in their own homes, depending on how far they had to travel. We worked these times throughout the winter of 1943 and on through 1944.

*

Due to the U-boat activity in the Atlantic we were experiencing severe losses of supply ships. Around this time I had a short conversation with Alan Clifton in the main corridor of Hursley House.

Joseph Smith came out of his office in a state of great excitement. He quickly checked that there was no one else about. Looking directly at me and grabbing Alan's hand, he burst out with the following words: 'I've just been told Station X have got the German Naval codes!' Without anything else being said I understood that this was an item of very secret information. He strode back into his office followed by Alan, who shut the door.

Thinking about this information on my way back to the Drawing Office, I realised I had been very privileged to hear this very secret news. It was obvious we now had access to all the German Naval messages, and perhaps our losses in the Atlantic Ocean would now be diminished. The story of the acquisition of these code books by the Royal Navy before the captured U-boat sank only became generally known years after the war.

Some 5,000 people were employed at Station X, and many of these were Wrens. The staff were able to decode the messages received and deliver them to a department where they were sent onward to those who required the knowledge – often within minutes of the messages being received and sometimes before the message had even arrived at its destination! Such was our people's speed and determination to beat the common enemy.

It was not until the 1990s that I discovered that Station X was the wartime code name for Bletchley Park.

*

In the summer of 1943 photographs were taken of the outside and inside of the experimental workshop where the Spiteful was in progress, and also of the inside and outside of the Drawing Office where my section can just be seen.

'Stella, you're having your photograph taken,' a colleague said as I was standing by his board. Looking up, I saw a flash from the far end of the hangar. This was most peculiar because we were supposed to be in a security zone!

Soon afterwards, while walking along a corridor in the house, I was grabbed by Alan Clifton with a message: 'Stella, YOU must be in this photograph.' I protested that I had already been photographed in the Drawing Office, but he brushed this aside, saying, 'Joseph commands you.' Taking me by the hand and saying 'Come on,' he escorted me past Joseph Smith and out of the front door. The visiting dignitaries, Joseph Smith, and management followed. Alan placed me in front of the personnel assembled from Supermarine Headquarters, next to Mr Gooch, who was leading the management to stand in the front row. Mr Gooch, who was very tall, moved half in front of me, so I had no option but to lean to one side and hold the arm of the girl next to me. This action can clearly be seen in the resultant photograph. IBM, who took over

Hursley House many years ago, published this group photograph in their house magazine. Photographs were also taken of the outside and inside of the Drawing Office and the experimental workshop near the Hursley gate. The interior photograph of the workshop shows the prototype of the Spiteful. These have been reproduced in *The Spitfire Story* by Alfred Price.

*

Jack Rasmussen was the representative of the Ministry of Aircraft Production. Having been appointed as the liaison officer to Supermarine, he had a desk in the newly built Drawing Office at Hursley.

One lunchtime, Gerry Gingell and I had returned early to the empty Drawing Office to listen to the news programme on his radio. As we listened, a figure appeared, making a beeline for us, and we were astonished to recognise Jack wearing RAF uniform! How could he have been called up? In reply to Gerry's query, he straightened his head and shoulders and declared with resignation, 'THEY have put me into uniform.'

Although we were wondering who 'they' might be, we knew better than to enquire further. Shaking hands and saying goodbye, we wished him good luck. We watched him disappear up the steps and out of sight, not knowing if we should ever see him again.

At a meeting of the Spitfire Society in the Hall of Aviation at Southampton on 15 November 1985, I met up with Jack again, and Kenneth Knell was also there. On a visit to Jack and his wife in 1994, I took the opportunity to ask him about the incident that took place on 1 June 1944. He consulted his diaries and, having checked his movements during May and June, gave me the following details:

On 1 May 1944 I went to Odiham to meet Group Captain Mayes of 84th Group 2nd TAC. Later I was interviewed at Hursley by an air vice marshal, who instructed me to hold myself in readiness for special duties. On the 1 June I was summoned to Odiham again and was put into RAF uniform. Before going home I had to call at Hursley to collect my belongings.

*

Making my way home at midday on Saturday 27 May 1944, I bypassed the village of Southwick. Cycling down a track beside a farmhouse, I turned on to the lane that led up to Fort Widley, and crossing a small bridge, turned sharp right to climb the hill. From the left-hand side of the road, two soldiers leapt out of the ditch in front of me, brandishing their rifles with fixed bayonets. What was I doing there? An officer was sent for, because I had to be taken into custody. He wanted to know how I had missed the road closure signs. Explaining that my usual route home across country was via the farmhouse track that bypassed Southwick, he immediately sent men to investigate and close the access.

On showing him my work pass with photograph, which was evidence of my employment with Supermarine, I begged to be allowed to continue my journey. If I had to go back to Southwick, cycle through Purbrook up the hill and down to Cosham, I would not arrive home for another three hours and my parents would be extremely worried and anxious. I stated further that I would not look to my left as I climbed Portsdown to pass Fort Widley and Fort Purbrook on my way to my home in Bedhampton.

Realising that I posed no threat to what was an obviously sensitive area, he let me go. Then I thought about Monday, saying,

'I will be coming back this way about 6 o-clock on Monday morning. You will not prevent me passing through, I hope, because I have to cycle 30 miles back to work?' He nodded, and his expression convinced me that all was well. On Monday I was rather apprehensive, and very much aware of the troops concealed at that corner, but they did not challenge me again.

Apparently Field Marshal Montgomery had arrived, and was in his caravan in the grounds of Broomfield House only yards from the corner. SHAEF (the Supreme Headquarters of the Allied Expeditionary Force) was in Southwick House just beyond. No wonder those lanes had been closed and were closely guarded!

6

SUPERMARINE MEMORIES

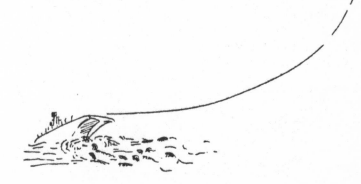

The next few sections document the stories and memories of several others who had close connections to Supermarine during the war.

Supermarine Memories: Jack Parnell

During the bombing of Southampton many civilians lost their homes. Jack Parnell and his family, among others, experienced more than one destruction. He tells his story as follows:

I joined Supermarine in 1935 and worked as a riveter in the tank shop (fuel) before being sent to the old roller mills on the western shore. By 1940 I was working in the Woolston works and still living with mother and brothers in Radstock Road. The sirens used to go off three or four times a day, and we just got on with our jobs between running up and down to the shelters. Once, cycling back from Denham with a mate, I saw a twin-engined plane flying up Southampton Water, obviously taking photographs of Supermarine. Another time an ME 109 hit a barrage balloon, which blew up, leaving just a wire!

One day my brother John and I were in our garden and although the weather was cloudy we could see the New Forest across Southampton Water. Coming towards us were several bombers, and we heard the click of their bomb doors opening as we dived into our shelter. The ground shook beneath us and we thought our house had gone, but we did not even have a broken window!

On Tuesday 24 September 1940 I had gone upstairs to have a bath when the sirens went off and bombs started dropping. Stark naked, I fled downstairs, and John threw his mac over me as we ran for our shelter. After the raid we found half the house had gone.

The bathroom had disappeared and it was impossible to get into my room. John climbed into mother's room and brought out some of her clothes and underwear for me to put on. Mother was in deep shock and stayed in the shelter until Gwen, my fiancée, arrived and we all went to Sydney's house (another brother).

The next day when the sirens went off and our guns opened up – there were no bombs! A single plane followed the river, obviously photographing the result of the previous day's attack on Supermarine.

Mother got another house, still in Radstock Road, and we moved everything we could salvage. Gwen and I were planning our marriage, and Sydney suggested it could take place from his house, but Mother was adamant. She stated 'No way. None of the others have. They will go from here', meaning Radstock Road. On the day itself, my sister's house was also bombed!

She and Mother decided to leave Southampton and move to a bungalow in Chandler's Ford. Gwen and I found a modern flat in Eastleigh. Our neighbour put mattresses into his lorry and took friends out to the country at night. When Eastleigh was bombed, one fell between our shelter and our neighbour's house, and we were buried alive! So we moved into the bungalow at

Chandler's Ford for a short time until Gwen and our son, then just six months old, went to live in Trowbridge with her parents. When D-Day started, we heard the transport planes going over all night.

Soon I was transferred to Trowbridge, and there we were far removed from the war. On going to work in the morning we met the night staff, who had beds made up in the canteen. We even had a chef to cook for us, and had our breakfast in the cookhouse. We returned to Southampton after the war, and two years later Norman (our brother) came home after having been a POW for six years.

I observed some American troops who were lined up in the market square; a sergeant was telling them what was happening. He said, 'Left turn. Off we go', and someone called out, 'Oh Sarg. We don't want to go that way. We went that way yesterday.' Can you imagine a British sergeant putting up with that? If he told you 'Left turn!', you did.

Mrs Morley, my wife's mother, lost her identity card, which meant she had to go to the civic centre in Southampton and apply for a new one. She was asked to give all the details and information for a new card to be issued, and when this had been done she was asked 'Have you anything to prove who you are?' She replied, 'Well, I've only got my identity card from the First World War.' Silence reigned until the officer said, 'Well we needn't have gone all through that Mrs Morley if you had shown me this card in the first place. I would have given you a new card straight away.' You see, all the identification was there. But fancy carrying a 1918 identity card in her handbag in the 1939 war! She had only taken it with her, just in case!

Supermarine Memories: Bill Fisher

Bill Fisher relates his time with Supermarine before the Second World War and the difficulties that the employees faced when the factory was bombed.

On leaving school in September 1938 a friend of my parents, Frank Wright, a fitter and shop steward at the Woolston works, arranged for me to have an interview with the foreman, Bill Crooks. He took me on as a night-shift worker and in the first year I had to do everything from helping fitters on double-handed jobs to cleaning out the hulls of the Walrus flying boats and making tea.

Work on the new factory, known at the Itchen works, had begun and as soon as the building was ready we all moved in. It was cold, as there were no tarpaulins on the waterfront side by the slipway. We had some braziers for warmth, but these were soon discontinued as the heat and fumes were harmful to the metal. One of my first jobs was to clean the wings of a number of Walrus flyingboats, still in silver colours. We also refurbished the Stranraers, two-engined flying boats, which were then painted in camouflage. Two experimental Spitfires on floats were built with the idea of using them in Norway, but I don't think they ever flew. Then I was set to work on Spitfire fuselages. As time went by everyone was aware that war was imminent, and we steadily increased production.

When war was declared we were enrolled in the LDVs – Local Defence Volunteers. Our uniform was just an armband, and some of us were picked to man the works' fire brigade. Later we became the Home Guard, and were issued with uniforms and a limited number of Lee Enfield rifles. There was an old Vickers water-cooled machine gun mounted in an old boat cabin on the railway embankment, and two men manned this all the time. Two Browning machine guns were mounted in sandbagged emplacements on the waterfront. We all took turns to do night patrols along the railway line as far as White's Yard, which could be scary. When it was thought we were going to be invaded we had one period of duty, which lasted twenty-four hours.

During the first few months of the war we had several scares. Everyone had to run to the shelters through a tunnel under the railway built behind the railway embankment. On Tuesday 24 September 1940 we sustained a heavy bombing attack. The factory was not badly hit, but the shelters and the nearby houses were bombed. My brother Frank had taken refuge with several others underneath the tunnel because they could not reach the shelters in time. He was lucky not to have been killed, as the railway received a direct hit and the embankment collapsed on top of them. Several people died in this attack, and Frank was buried up to his shoulders and suffered a compound fracture of his leg among other injuries.

That night when we reported for duty we were told that the staff had already moved out to the Polygon Hotel. As no lights could be used due to bomb damage, this meant we could not conform to the black-out regulations. Now our job was to come in the next morning and help clear up. Everyone was apprehensive, but Wednesday passed relatively quietly. Lord Beaverbrook, Minister for Aircraft Production, appeared and gave Supermarine *carte blanche* to commandeer any garage, laundry or building anywhere that might be considered suitable for the production of Spitfires.

By mid-afternoon on Thursday we had moved virtually everything to other sites. Then the warning to take cover sounded and with Ted Bridges, one of the charge hands, we ran through the gap in the embankment, now cleared, to the first shelter. Inside, he turned to me and said, 'There are too many in here, we'll find another.' Running to the next one, we found only a few people inside. Then the bombs started dropping all around and the gunners on Peartree Green were firing their Bofors non-stop, which was a comfort to us. Our shelter had a near miss; the blast blew the metal escape hatch off the roof and the concrete floor cracked. To ease our fear we swore and cursed the German pilots. At last we heard the all clear. No one in our shelter was hurt, but we were all badly shaken.

Outside, the place was a shambles. The shelters had been built on soft soil, which may have saved some lives, but it was a mud-and-clay quagmire. The shelter that Ted and I had first gone into was badly damaged, and our work mates were climbing out, many with severe injuries. We did what we could to help until the first aid people arrived and took over. One young lad was badly shocked, and I was asked to see he got home to Hythe. Taking him to our house in Bitterne, I made him a cup of tea, and when he had calmed down I walked with him to Whites Road to catch a bus.

As my wife was not at home I went to the Merry Oak estate, thinking she would be with my parents, but my elder brother was the only person there. He told me my wife and sister had gone to visit my younger brother in the Royal South Hampshire Hospital in St Mary's Road. Eventually we all met up and I heard that they had been in a shelter in the town and someone had told them that Vickers Supermarine had been wiped out. They were so relieved to see me, even though I was covered in mud.

Back at the factory many people were trying to clear up the mess, and I was told to find my tools, if they were still there, and report the next day to Hendy's garage at the back of Woolworth's.

We worked there for a few weeks until Southampton had a blitz. Hendy's had no electric power, so I was sent to Seward's garage on the Winchester road and shortly afterwards I was transferred to Reading.

Our house was damaged in the blitz, so after putting our furniture into store with a farmer on the Durley road, we went into lodgings with a couple of farm workers. When the specially built factory at Caversham Heights was ready everyone transferred there. Mr Weedy, who had been in the K shop at Woolston, was put in charge. Mary and I moved into a large house converted by the local authority into flats. Bungalows that were being built by the Ministry of Aircraft Production especially for the Supermarine workers in Northumberland Avenue were just like those built at Ampfield near Hursley.

During this time some of us had to go to Benson Airfield near Oxford to convert the fighter fuselages into photographic reconnaissance aircraft. Virtually all the members of the original team at Supermarine spent a lot of time acting as 'teachers', instructing unskilled workers in this modification. There were so many cameras to be fitted that we had to reroute all the flying control cables. A tricky job. When a red alert sounded I was working inside the tail portion, and how I got out of the small square door I cannot remember. But I was fairly slim. Our nearest shelters were holes in the ground covered with planks of wood and turf on top. One raider dropped oil bombs, and one fell underneath a Wellington bomber nearby; seconds later it went up in flames.

Before the war a Spitfire (K 9834) had been built at Eastleigh and prepared for the world land plane speed record. It had no armament, and gleamed with many coats of blue paint with a white flash along the side. It was decommissioned when the war started, and in November 1940 was given to the photographic reconnaissance unit at Benson. Wing Commander Geoffrey Tuttle and later his successor, Air Commodore John Boothman, both flew this machine. It was fortunate that on a previous occasion our Commanding Officer had been able to get this Spitfire up and well away before the raiders arrived.

Supermarine Memories: Ken Miles and Lord Beaverbrook to the Rescue

The following article is the recollections of Ken Miles's life with Supermarine when he called Lord Beaverbrook for help.

When the war started in 1939 my father, a shopkeeper, thought I should leave school and get a job. Having received a good business education he naturally thought I should get a job in business, but I wanted to be an engineer like my uncle. He was very disappointed but he agreed to my wishes. The first man who came into father's shop wearing dirty overalls was asked if he could get me a job, which he very kindly did – working in a garage.

One evening I came home in a filthy mess after having spent the day crawling under cars. My uncle said, 'Good Lord, what on earth have you been doing?' Proudly I told him I was now working in a garage as an engineer. He was extremely annoyed with father and told him I had not received a secondary education to become a motor mechanic which, although an honourable job, was not the place in which to train as an engineer.

My uncle was a staunch Union supporter and brought the matter up at their next meeting. They invited me to attend and asked if I would like an apprenticeship with Supermarine. Such was the power of the Union that an interview was immediately forthcoming. There I was told the company was not taking on any more apprentices but in view of my education I could start at Eastleigh works on the following Monday, and when I became sixteen I could begin as an apprentice aircraft fitter. I was thrilled to be working, earning 2½d per hour on the final assembly of the famous Spitfire.

One day a boy came up to me and asked if I was an apprentice. I told him I was an apprentice aircraft fitter, at which he said 'Oh' and walked away. 'That's strange,' I thought and went after him.

'What do you mean, Oh?'

'Oh nothing,' he replied.

So I asked him the same question.

'Oh, I'm an apprentice aircraft engineer.'

'What's the difference?' I asked.

'Oh well, you will be just a fitter when you have finished your apprenticeship but I shall be on the design or technical staff.'

Thinking things over I decided that I did not want to be an aircraft fitter but an aircraft engineer, so banged on the door of Mr Nelson, the Manager.

'Come in!' he shouted.

'What do you want?'

'I want to be an aircraft engineer not a fitter.'

'Don't be silly,' he said, 'You're going to be a fitter and that's that.'

Then he threw me out of the office. I kept thinking about the matter and the next day I knocked on Mr Nelson's door again and told him I wanted to see Mr Pratt, the General Manager. 'What for?' he said.

'I want my apprenticeship changed to aircraft engineer,' whereupon I was practically booted out of the office. I stewed about this for days, thinking as to how I could get to see Mr Pratt.

All kinds of visitors came to see the new version of the Spitfire, which was being assembled by a few selected workmen. A few days later a large limousine arrived with several people from the government, including Mr Quill, the test pilot; Mr Richardson, the Chief Inspector; and several high-ranking RAF officers. They gathered around the new aircraft, some standing on the wing and others on a platform that had been erected at the side. I knew Mr Quill and Mr Richardson by sight so I asked another boy who the others were. He pointed out Mr Pratt but did not know anyone else. Mr Pratt, I thought, that's the man I need to see. Without a moment's thought I climbed on the wing and tapped Mr Pratt on the shoulder.

'Yes yes?' he said.

'I want to be an aircraft engineer.'

Everybody laughed and two security men grabbed me off the wing.

After they left I was called into Mr Nelson's office and he gave me a terrible ticking off, asking me if I hadn't been taught any manners at my 'posh' school. 'Well,' I said 'You wouldn't let me see Mr Pratt,' and once again I was thrown out. Two days afterwards I was called into Mr Nelson's office once more, and this time I was sure that I was going to be given the sack. 'You've caused some trouble you have lad,' he said. 'There's a car outside. Mr Elliott the Assistant General Manager wants to see you.' At Woolston, in Mr Elliott's office, I was given another dressing down.

'What's all this about anyway?'

I told him I wanted my apprenticeship changed from fitter to engineer. He said I did not have enough qualifications and I was sent back to Eastleigh, where Mr Nelson stated he didn't want to hear any more of the matter. I was very despondent and felt utterly miserable.

To my horror I was summoned to Mr Nelson's office again.

'The matter is not over yet my lad, Mr Daniel wants to see you.'

He was the employment officer and at that time also acted as apprentice supervisor. Having met him when I first started work at Supermarine, I found him to be a very kind man. This is it, I thought, my employment is no longer required. At Woolston I was escorted to his office and there he told me he had been informed of my behaviour and that I did not have enough qualifications to train as an aircraft engineer. I stated if I had not left school early in order to get an apprenticeship, I was sure I would have obtained the necessary qualifications. Having given the matter some thought he said that although I had caused a lot of trouble he admired my tenacity. I was to attend a work school, which was being set up to raise the education of the shop boys. They did the same work as the apprentices but did not move around to learn other skills. After three months he would assess my progress, and if he found it was satisfactory he would break all precedence and change my indentures to aircraft engineer.

None of the boys attending this school had the advantages of a secondary education; consequently I was far ahead of the others at the end of three months. My indentures were changed to aircraft engineer. I had made myself noticed, had stood firm with determination and had got to where I wanted to be.

In 1940 my parents went to live with some relatives to escape the constant night bombing. Businesses at that time had to have a firewatcher at night, so father put up a bunk bed behind the shop for me. When the shop was bomb damaged with slates blown off and windows shattered I went to live with friends in Romsey. From there I could still commute to Eastleigh.

The Cunliffe Owen factory was next to the Supermarine works at Eastleigh. When the sirens sounded we all ran to the shelters on the opposite side of the main road. After the 'all clear' we saw a pall of black smoke over the Cunliffe Owen factory, and I lost my best friend in that raid. Afterwards, dummy guns were made from metal tubes, and these were put around the hangars at Eastleigh to deter any further dive-bombers.

When the main Supermarine works was bombed, volunteers were asked to report to the office. As I had trained in first aid I went along, only to be told I was too young. I was sixteen! Mr Bartholomew, my charge hand, had sent his family into the country, but he was killed when a stray bomb fell on his house. His wife asked that his tools be given to an apprentice and they were given to me.

On 3 June 1941 I was transferred to Hursley Park. It was a large country estate owned by Commander Bird and had been taken over by Supermarine after the Woolston works had been destroyed as their headquarters. In the garage, which had previously held limousines, benches were set up for the experimental workshop. Under the archway we worked on an experimental Spitfire fuselage until our work was transferred to the new hangar by the main gate. The day the transfer took place, several of us were delegated to carry this fuselage to the new hangar. It was lifted on to our shoulders and we proceeded to walk the half-mile to our new home. Our way took us through the orchard and when we arrived the fuselage was full of apples.

On 22 March 1943 I was transferred to Sewards, which was one of the dispersal units. It had been a local garage before it was commandeered by Supermarine. I was to report to Mr Dicky Earl, who was foreman of the jig and tool department. He was an old employee and well respected, although a bit of a character. Outside his office I waited for him to arrive and he greeted me by asking, 'What is that box for?' I explained it was my tool box, to which he replied, 'You won't be needing that for the job you are going to do. You are to take over the Drawing Office.' I laughed, saying he must have mistaken me for someone else. But no. On introduction to the draughtsman, I explained I did not know anything about drawing, but was told that as he was joining the Air Force the following week I was to take over his job. He showed me the work I was expected to do, which was to make drawings of tools and jigs. Some were drawn from tools made in the tool room and others I had to design myself.

'I can't do that.' I said.

'Well, that's what your job is going to be' was the answer.

Apparently the management had assessed my potential and decided that I would be suitable to join the design staff at some future date. I had just two weeks to learn the basics before the other man left.

One day I was told a car was waiting to take me to Hursley to meet Mr Lennox Taylor, who had been appointed apprentice supervisor. He confided to me that the Earl of Gainsborough was to start work at Supermarine. 'I know what you lads are with new boys and I want you to do your best to look after him, but on no account must other boys be told that he is an earl.' Promising to respect his confidence I returned to my office, but another apprentice came up to me asking if I knew a real live earl was starting. Some secret! Later Tony Gainsborough was transferred to Hursley Drawing Office in the electrical section.

Mr Gooch, the general works manager, told me to go to Trowbridge and learn the Robinson Process. After many months in the tool room drawing office I was reasonably confident in my ability to draw. The process was to draw on matt, grey, plated aluminium sheet, and these drawings had to be accurate to within a 5000th of an inch. These would be sent to the works and used as a template. I took great care with my first drawing, never before having had to be so accurate, and submitted it to Mr Wills, the inspector. He rejected my drawing as it was not within the permitted tolerance. I did it again only to have it rejected a second time. After three rejections I was pretty fed up and just wanted to return to my office at Sewards. A kindly senior draughtsman, seeing my misery, asked if he could help. On explaining the problem he looked at my rule, which was the usual draughtsman's wooden rule, and told me it would be impossible to draw to the required limits with it. He showed me the correct type, which was stainless steel and graduated to a 100th of an inch. With a magnifying glass and a chisel-pointed 4H pencil, you could pinpoint a position roughly halfway between the 100th graduations, and that would be within the required tolerance.

The next day I called at Lawsons, our local tool shop, and asked for a Chesterman No. 761/3 rule. The salesman laughed and said such a thing had not been seen since the start of the war and was unattainable. How was I expected to help the war effort if I could not get the tool to do the job? Who could help me find one? Lord Beaverbook, the Minister for Aircraft Production, would probably know, so I wrote to him. I received his very nice reply, which told me to return to Lawsons where a rule would be waiting. You can imagine the surprise that Lawsons must have had!

I was not happy at Trowbridge and did not get on too well with the boss. One problem was that I was a member of 'staff' and he was still considered 'works'. So at lunchtimes he would have to go into the works canteen while I went to the staff one. Out of work we got on fine, and the young lady I met in the office, later to be my wife, and I were often asked to tea at his house. Although he was well respected as a loftsman, I found him a bad administrator and made it obvious. Coming from a young lad, this did not go down so well. Eventually I was reported to Mr Lennox Taylor, who put me back on tools and sent me to Shorts in Winchester.

A couple of weeks after starting, on 14 August 1944, the works manager called me into his office and said, 'You're a draughtsman aren't you? I understand you used to run a drawing office at Sewards.' I acknowledged that I had been doing drawings but that I wouldn't call myself a draughtsman, and he went on to say, 'I want to start one here, would you run it?' I agreed to set up an office and was shown a room with just a table and chair. He agreed I could go to Hursley to get a drawing board, tee square and some other items, which I managed to get from Mr Richardson, who was in charge of the tool drawing office.

I worked in this office for several months until Mr Lennox Taylor heard of it. On being summoned to his office, I was greeted with the words,

'You are supposed to be back on your tools.'

I replied it was not my fault – I was told to do it.

'I'm not having this!' he stormed, 'Back on your tools you were sent and that is where you are staying.'

So I was sent to Lowthers in Southampton on 19 November 1944 and put to work on a milling machine. Three weeks later he sent for me again. Now what have I done? I thought.

'I can't keep you out of a drawing office, can I?' he said. 'You are to start in the Drawing Office at Hendys, Chandlers Ford next week.'

The liaison officer was Dave Sidley, a draughtsman from Hursley who set me to work drawing details supplied by him. Soon I was accepted as his assistant, often going to the various dispersal units to sort out problems. At this point I was still 'works' but on 19 April 1945 I was promoted to 'staff'. I was on my way back!

Transferred to Hursley Drawing Office on 9 August, I continued to work under Dave until loaned to Mr Richardson, the manager at South Marston, to set up a small drawing office on 26 March 1946. There I lived in a hotel and dined with senior staff. Then Mr Lovell-Cooper, having had good reports of my work, requested my return to Hursley. Mr Richardson kept getting it postponed, but eventually I had to go back.

At Hursley I found that the 'Glass House' [where the women tracers of the DO worked], so-called because of the secrecy of the work there, had been enlarged. Under the supervision of Jack Davis, a senior section leader, I was to design part of the undercarriage locking system for the Swift. It was very satisfying to see it set up in a rig being raised and lowered, proving my design worked satisfactorily.

My father, still running his small electronic component business, kept asking me to join him as he was in poor health. I was not interested as he would not have been able to pay the same wage as Supermarine, and anyway I knew nothing about electronics. When he became very ill and had to enter hospital he asked me to look after the business. Mr Lovell-Cooper very kindly offered to give me leave of absence when I explained the situation, but I was back at Hursley six weeks later. Shortly afterwards, father was taken into hospital again. I explained to Mr Cooper that I would have to resign because mother's livelihood depended on the business. He was very understanding and said he was sorry I had to go, but if I wanted to come back at any time I would be welcome, providing it was not too long. I left Supermarine on 18 April 1948 never to return.

My father died and I was left to run a business about which I knew very little. After years of struggle, having successfully expanded the business I sold it to a national company before retiring, but that's another story.

During my apprenticeship I experienced many unusual events. Dicky Bird, the son of Commander Bird, the previous owner of Supermarine, worked for a while at the Eastleigh works and kept his light aircraft inside one of the hangars. One day I was told to help him. He explained that he would start it and I was to swing the propeller. I was dead scared and after several failed attempts Dicky told me to get in the cockpit, press a button, shout 'contact', he would swing the propeller and I was to press another button. All went well until it started to taxi towards the hangar. Dicky grabbed a wing and jumped up into the cockpit and switched the engine off. I was not asked to help again.

On the grass just outside the main hangar the apprentices used to play football, and Jeffrey Quill and Alex Henshaw, the test pilots, often flew their test flights low over our heads. [Alex has confirmed this fact to the author.]

The old S6A Schneider trophy plane hung in the roof of the hangar at Eastleigh. The apprentices were given the job of preparing it to be used in the film *The Life of Mitchell* starring Leslie Howard. Afterwards it was put on display at the Royal Pier before finally being laid to rest in the local museum.

Another film was being made about this time, called, I believe, *Men Behind the Guns*. The camera crew came to Eastleigh and shot various processes, one of which was of me working on the undercarriage system. My parents were very excited and when the film came out we all went to see it but my piece had been cut!

Dr Horace King, a friend of my parents, wrote a song called 'The Hampshire Spitfire Song'. Copies of this song were given to the staff at Eastleigh, but it seems these have all disappeared, including mine. The sale of this sheet music was designed to raise cash for the Spitfire Fund. Any town wishing to help was given permission to insert their own name in place of 'Hampshire'. Dr King was later a Speaker of the House of Commons, then became Lord Maybray King of the House of Lords. [Since meeting with Ken, the author has acquired a copy of the words and music from the archives of the *Hampshire Chronicle*, who received it from the Eastleigh and District Local History Society.]

Early on in the Battle of Britain some men from the Royal Air Force came to Eastleigh to give us a course of instruction on servicing Browning machine guns. Working on a bench opposite a Spitfire set up on trestles for minor repair work, someone got in the cockpit and pressed the firing button. This was common practice to blow out the system, but on this occasion bullets had been left up the spout! There was a terrific bang and bullets shot just over my head into the electrical conduit, causing a small fire and fusing all the lights. A workman who had been leaning on the wing between the guns dropped to the ground and we all thought he had been shot, but I think he was in a dead faint.

Supermarine After 1949: Alf Shorter

These are the memories of Alf Shorter, relating his employment with Folland Aircraft where they were producing the Gnat, his work at Supermarine and his life.

After seven years of cycling 6 miles each way to work every day, I decided to make a change. On 1 January 1956, I joined Vickers Armstrong's Supermarine works at Woolston, Southampton, where my brothers were already working. When the Scimitar programme ended, nearly everyone had to learn new skills for the nuclear submarine space models. I remember with pleasure that I could mark out, cut, roll and weld a lobster-back bend. Other devices were later manufactured for the nuclear programme. The new work demanded a great deal of skill and the use of entirely new materials.

The manufacture of Magnox fuel channel sleeves was one job in which I was involved. There were also monstrous radiation shields in the form of steel tubes around 1 foot in diameter. These were filled with chilled cast iron and concrete, loaded into a strongback, then upended and secured into a huge ballrace situated in the roof trusses of the hangar. These were then rotated and checked for straightness. The jobs that we were required to do were far removed from any that were previously used in aircraft construction. In spite of the difficulty of the work I cannot recall anyone who lacked enthusiasm to tackle the challenges with which we were presented.

My working life ended in a local engineering firm where I was in charge of the inspection department. One day the quality manager brought three young lads to me who were participating in the youth training scheme. While giving them basic information, I was surprised to be interrupted with the question 'Where are our chairs?' Has the respect that was given to senior managers in my youth changed so dramatically to this causal attitude to work?

During the miners' strike I became tired of the television media interviews stressing how hard done by they were, when these were often carried out in working men's clubs where all and sundry were drinking ale and smoking like factory chimneys.

I know that I am an intolerant old man who thinks, as did Oscar Wilde, that youth is wasted on young people. But think on; the basic rate of pay in the fifties was about £12 per week and this was considered good money, although the majority of my acquaintances could not afford a car. Cycle racks were more important to the average working man. Perhaps this is why we now have the problem of unemployment.

One incident I recall from my days at Supermarine was on a Sunday afternoon when the charge hand came to tell me that my son, a police cadet, had just come off duty and wanted to see me.

'What's up lad?' I asked him.

'The line pole has broken' was his reply. (Note: line pole = telegraph pole.)

'You haven't come down here to tell me that!' I said.

I was earning double pay for the day, plus a 150 per cent bonus, so I wasn't too pleased to be called out for what I considered was a very minor problem.

'Ah! But it fell across the greenhouse' was the next piece of information.

After a short silence my son added, 'Mum was in the greenhouse.'

Dropping everything, I hurried home to find my wife still in one piece but considerably shaken by her experience.

7

TOMORROW IS D-DAY

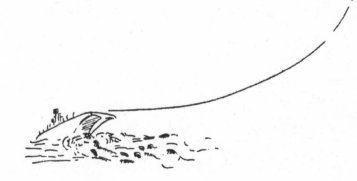

TOMORROW IS D-DAY

This is the true story of what took place during the evening before the D-Day invasion of Normandy.

General Eisenhower and General Montgomery decided to hold a farewell party on Saturday 3 June 1944, the night before the invasion of Normandy. This was to be hosted by Major General Douglas Graham at his headquarters in a Nissen hut in the forest of Hursley Park.

General Montgomery contacted Joseph Smith, Chief Designer of Supermarine, as to whether he could recommend a lady who could be trusted with regards to security. His reply was that, yes, there was one lady – Stella Broughton. He had observed her to be circumspective, trustworthy and security conscious in her work for the design of the Spitfire and Spiteful.

During the afternoon of Wednesday 31 May, on instructions from General Montgomery, Major General Graham visited Joseph Smith's office in Hursley Park House. His remit was to discover if I could cope with being a hostess to a large number of officers.

Gerald Gingell, section leader of Technical Publications, was summoned and asked his opinion of me. Could Stella cope with a large group of men? He replied that she was the only female in a Drawing Office with a hundred men, her demeanour was always correct and her immediate colleagues were happy to have her on their team. (These remarks were related to me many days later by Alan Clifton, Joseph Smith's deputy.)

On returning to the Drawing Office, Gerald came to my desk looking very agitated and asked belligerently, 'What have YOU been up to?' Startled, I said, 'What are you talking about?' He went on to say that he'd been asked some very searching questions about me. He pressed me further, but what could I say? I really had no idea what this was about.

We racked our brains and concluded the only thing to do was wait and see what might develop. Understandably, I felt there must be something in this. Indeed it was not until I was compiling dates for my book that the above incident came to mind, and this, coupled with what was to follow, made me realise that an Army intelligence investigation as to my ability to act as hostess to a large number of men had been carried out.

At 10.15 a.m. on Saturday 3 June 1944, a shaft of sunlight fell across my board, sending a brilliant white reflection into my eyes. Bother, I thought, now the ink will dry too quickly and these curves are so tricky to do. Moving so that the shadow of my head covered my work, I became aware that Joseph Smith and a military officer had entered the hangar and were approaching the Chief Draughtsman's office. Being used to a variety of visitors to the Drawing Office I did not take any further interest in their arrival, so when Gerry paused by my desk shortly afterwards I was very surprised to hear him say, 'Stella, you're wanted in Mr Cooper's office.'

Speeding to the cloakroom to wash the ink off my fingers, I wondered what this summons could mean. Saturday morning! Oh no! It must be they wanted me to work overtime. I hadn't planned anything special for the weekend, except to visit the cinema. Making my way between the desks and along the main gangway, I saw Joseph Smith disappearing out of the hangar doors. Turning towards the Chief's office I felt, rather than saw, many pairs of eyes swivelling in my direction. Eyes, always watching, always curious, wondering what I was doing. Is it because I'm a girl? I thought. Well, carry on being curious, you'll not find out from me.

Knocking on the open door, I stepped into Mr Cooper's office.

'Good morning, Sir. I understand you wanted to see me?'

'Yes, Miss Broughton. Come in and close the door please.' His manner and voice were exceptionally cordial, different from his usual bark, and was that really a smile? Although he demanded respect and immediate attention to his orders, I had never felt intimidated by his attitude, which was his way of dealing with the pressure of work and getting the best out of his staff of some 200 men. He waved a hand to the chair in front of his desk, so I sat down, waiting to hear why I had been summoned.

Leaning forward, he asked in a hesitant manner, 'Are you doing anything particular this afternoon?' Here we go, I thought, what's up now? And what's HE doing here? I wondered, catching sight of the military officer seated on a low chair in the corner, for I had assumed he had left with Joseph Smith.

'Nothing in particular, Sir. I'm not going home this weekend. Do you want me to come in?'

'No, no.' he replied. 'Not to work, but we wondered...' and he turned to the officer, clearly uncertain how to continue, '... if you would be kind enough to accept an invitation to a party tonight?'

'A party? Tonight?' I exclaimed. Thoughts flashed through my mind – why me? Surely only senior staff warranted this sort of invitation?

Feeling stunned and thoroughly bemused, I found I was being introduced to Major General Graham. He had drawn closer to the desk and was shaking my hand, saying, 'I would be delighted if you would honour me with your company this evening as my personal guest. The party is to celebrate the opening of a new officers' mess in the camp and I would like you to act as my hostess.'

Mr Cooper, having done his job of introduction, had sat back in his chair and was beaming benevolently at my obvious astonishment. To gain time I thanked him slowly, thinking, could I have heard correctly? Hostess? Its meaning in those days was rather risqué, but both Mr Smith and Mr Cooper appeared to think everything was all right, otherwise they would not have introduced this officer. Therefore, as it had been approved by the head of the firm, I could accept this unusual invitation. So I replied, 'Thank you very much, I will be delighted to come.'

Pausing, I was appalled to realise that I had no evening dress in my limited wardrobe at my digs, although I did have my gold dancing sandals. Hastily assessing the number of clothing coupons in my book and the amount of money in my bank account I continued, 'But I have no evening dress with me. I don't know if I can get one this afternoon.' He hastened to assure me that it was not to be a formal affair, so I said, 'Oh, in that case I have a yellow day dress, would that do?' He appeared to freeze. His eyes glazed over and the thought came to me that he might think it was the ghastly lime yellow currently in fashion, which he absolutely abhorred. This caused me to comment further, 'It's an old gold colour.' At this, his eyes refocused on mine and he said in a very quiet and controlled voice, 'That would be most suitable.' Just how suitable it was, I was not to know until much later.

'Might I ask how many other ladies will be there?' I asked, and I was told he hoped there would be several, one being a lady who worked in the main house, along with some American ladies. Problems of access made me enquire, 'How shall I be able to get there and into the camp?' Thoughts crossed my mind of the almost non-existent bus service, and the noticeboard that could be seen along the road stating 'Civilians are forbidden to loiter or talk to the troops', plus the announcement that all military camps were sealed and no one was allowed in or out. Quickly he explained, 'I shall send my jeep and the driver will have a special pass for you.' I was still not completely happy.

'Yes, but will it get me out again? The camp is sealed is it not? I must be able to get back here for Monday morning.' I was thinking of the complicated and unfinished drawing on my board that a dispatch rider was due to collect by midday.

He smiled and said quietly, 'I am the Senior British Commanding Officer and no one goes in or out of any camp without my personal signature.'

Being confident all my queries had been resolved, I asked him what time he wanted me to be ready to be picked up. 'Would seven o'clock be too early? And may I have your address?' Mr Cooper handed him pen and paper, and these details were quickly written down. A final handshake, a brief 'thank you' to Mr Cooper, and I left the office.

Back at my desk, I was able to say to those who wanted to know what was going on that I had been invited to a party. No need to say where, with whom or even when. Fortunately by lunchtime everyone was dashing off to their homes for the weekend break, and had no time to question me further.

That afternoon while pressing my dress and making a gold headband from some velvet ribbon to match, I thought through the morning's conversation in Mr Cooper's office. 'That would be most suitable.' What a very strange remark the General had made about the colour of my dress. Not what one would normally expect from a mature military gentleman to an unknown twenty-year-old girl. Very peculiar!

I wondered how I had come to have been recommended to be the General's guest. It must have been Joseph Smith. Security was obviously the primary factor, for the door to Mr Cooper's office, which was always left open unless Joseph Smith was present or I was being given an assignment, had been closed. Mr Smith and Mr Cooper knew that I had always worked in predominately male situations and that I could cope with aplomb in the present Drawing Office of some 200 men. They were also aware that I had signed the Official Secrets Act, not once, but twice. It was possible that Jack Rasmussen, the representative of the Ministry of Aircraft Production at Hursley, who acted as a liaison officer, may have been consulted, as he knew me very well. I came to the conclusion that the reason for the party was not entirely correct; it was a cover for something more important.

*

'Here it comes!' cried one of the twins, and all three made a beeline for the hall, only to be held back with the raised finger of Mrs Ward, who said firmly, 'Stay put.' So when the knock came I indicated to her that she should open the door, not me, after all it was her house. I was just the lodger. Unknown to either of us, the eldest boy, David, had quietly whisked out of the back door and when I got to the front gate, there he was courteously holding it open and wishing me 'good evening', much to the amusement of the driver. I did not know until some forty-six years later that David had recorded all the names of the jeeps he saw. There were only two that had entered our close and apparently this one was named either *Clarence* or *Diarrhoea*! Could the latter have been indicative of the commander in the field going through the battle zones like a dose of salts? Can anyone tell me?

I had never ridden in a jeep before, and this was an American vehicle so I took notice of the driver's advice to sit in the middle of the rear seat. Even then it was not exactly a smooth ride, being both noisy and chilly, as the weather was distinctly cool for the time of the year. I was very glad of my yellow-and-brown tweed jacket.

At the gate to the estate the driver presented his credentials and the authorisation paper for my entry. The guards were not at all happy to let me through, so I took out my works pass which included a photograph, and told them that as this was my place of work they could not refuse my entry. We were then allowed to proceed. Following the road past Hursley House, we turned up the hill towards the edge of the woods. Here, there was an 8-foot-high mesh fence and a heavily guarded gate. The jeep stopped and as the driver pulled on the brakes, two hands appeared above him, grabbed him by the shoulders and heaved him out of the jeep to disappear from view into the darkness. At the same time, two soldiers brandishing drawn bayonets swept close on each side – those shining blades were within inches of my face. I froze. One soldier said to the other in a strong cockney accent, 'What's she doin' 'ere? She can't come in 'ere.'

I remained glued to my seat, not daring to do other than to look straight ahead. It seemed an interminable time before my driver was released and we were allowed to go on. Apparently the guards had been changed after my driver had passed on his way out, and they had to send for an officer to confirm the signature and instruction on the document signed by the General.

Thinking this was the last checkpoint, I was surprised to find we were approaching yet a third gate. Here our reception was less traumatic. Even though my driver was known personally to the guards on this gate, we were still not allowed through until our passes had been checked by another officer. Finally the jeep roared up the steep track to the top of the hill and came to a stop outside a Nissen hut tucked underneath the shade of the overhanging trees. My driver requested that I remain in the jeep while he went inside. A few moments later the General came out and escorted me past the two MPs who were standing on guard at the doorway.

At first the bright light dazzled me, but I was drawn to one side and introduced to some of the Major General's staff. He took my jacket and gave it to one of them with the instruction to put it in his quarters. Turning around, I was met with the sight of a magnificent buffet, where some waiters were busy putting the last-minute touches to an array of such quantity and rarity in those days of rationing that I stared in amazement and scarcely took in the arrangements of the tables and the bandsmen trying out their instruments. The buffet was made up of some five trestles covered with pristine white cloths, decorated with greenery and loaded with every conceivable culinary delight. There were whole roasted chickens, a baron of beef, a whole leg of lamb and a huge joint of pork. Bowls of fruit salad, jugs of cream, iced cakes, sausage rolls, apples, pears and wonder of all, a hand of bananas! Further along were bottles of different brands of whisky and gin, wine and liqueurs as well as fruit juices and numerous cans of beer.

It was obvious that the American sector must have supplied many items as their contribution to the party. Bananas had not been seen in the shops for a very long time, and oranges only spasmodically. Along the rear wall were the stands and instruments for the band. On the left-hand side, tables had been set up end-on to the wall, with stools on either side. The perfectly polished wood reflected the gleaming cutlery and coloured serviettes, giving an atmosphere that was both stimulating and exciting. How could I ever forget this scene? Parties were but memories of childhood in my experience.

We started to walk down the centre of the hut and stopped by the side of a table, where a white-coated waiter was laying up with his back towards us. 'Would you please leave that,' said the Major General. Startled, the man turned at this request and stammered, 'I'm sorry, Sir, I haven't finished yet.' The short command 'Out' and a jerk of his thumb sent the waiter, with a deferential 'Yes, Sir', scuttling rapidly for the door.

Taken aback at this curt command, I glanced back and was astonished to discover that the hut was empty of all those who had been milling around on my arrival. The doorway was completely blocked by the backs of the two Red Caps. Obviously the order had been given that when the lady guest arrived everyone was to leave.

Major General Graham turned to me and said, 'Tomorrow is D-Day. That is why you have been requested to be the hostess this evening. I paid great attention as he proceeded to outline what General Eisenhower and General Montgomery required me to do to make the evening a success. My presence as a civilian in the environment of this secluded camp was to bring an element of normal everyday life to the event for all the officers who had been ordered to attend. The idea was that the event would mean that all the senior officers could recognise each other during the coming invasion of Brittany. He told me that such as event had never been held before a major battle. My job was to greet them, and to get them to relax, eat some food and chat together so that they would sleep that night.

All the officers were expected to spend at least ten minutes, and preferably half an hour, in my company. This had been put to them as a request, but it was virtually an order. He then went on to mention possible incidents that might occur, and hoped I would be able to cover any possible effects on the officers.

As I have been blessed with a photographic memory, his words have been seared into my brain.

Then he asked, on behalf of General Montgomery, for my agreement to the following: I was not to reveal any information about this event until sixty-odd years had passed, to which I agreed. (Reader, please note I had signed the Secrets Act for both the Navy and the Air Force, and my security level was such that to sign again for the Army was not required.)

He finished the five-minute briefing by apologising in advance for not being able to stay by my side for much of the time, as he wanted to make sure that everyone came into the mess. He expressed the hope that I would enjoy the food, drink and music, and he would make sure I was escorted home at the end of the evening. I said I had understood all his instructions and, thanking him once again for his invitation, promised to do my best to make it a memorable evening.

Leaving me in the centre of the hut, he spoke to the Red Caps, who moved away, and in poured the 'team', who quickly finished their final preparations just in time for the first arrivals. From then onwards Major General Graham was kept very busy greeting everyone at the door and then bringing them to be introduced to me. Every officer was from a different regiment or unit. They were introduced by their correct rank, but having little knowledge of military titles, I chose to address each as 'Mister', which enabled me to avoid a faux pas. This was instinctive on my part, but with hindsight it proved to be the best thing to have done, for the evening became more of a private party, irrespective of any military overtones. Just what the General wished to achieve, *n'est pas*?

Some time later, having noted that I was coping with the continuous flow of visitors, he kept disappearing and then returning with another officer in tow. One of them in answer to the question as to what he would like to eat, said, 'Oh I don't think I really want anything.' Expressing surprise, I showed him what a variety of food was displayed, and because of my attitude he took some food and sat down with me and talked. I was aware that Major General Graham was very pleased with this reaction.

Shortly afterwards, he came to my side, saying how pleasantly surprised he was at the unexpected arrival of some senior American officers, and would I come with him to meet them. As we crossed the room he spoke to me, saying, 'This is Lt General Omar Bradley, but his rank is the equivalent of mine.' As American names were unfamiliar to me, this name eluded me for years until I discovered that there was no other American officer of that particular rank on that day.

I was introduced, and he took my hand and was profuse in his thanks for my being present that evening. But while we were talking he would not let go, and instead placed both hands around mine and kept them there. At first I thought he might be drunk, but then I realised he was holding on to me as though in sheer relief at being able to be close to someone, so I did not draw away. After a few minutes he turned and introduced the other American officer as Major General Clarence Huebner, who likewise expressed his thanks for my attendance. He appeared to be very calm, but was keeping his feelings under tight control. The name of Huebner sounded to me like a flowing river, and I never forgot it. As we now know, Lt General Omar Bradley was in command of the First US Army and Major General Clarence Huebner was in command of the 1st US Division. Shortly afterwards they took their leave, as they had a long journey to get back to their ship before midnight.

As they left, the General took me over to the other side of the room to be introduced to three other senior officers. The first was Major General Rodney Keller, who was in command of the 3rd Canadian Division, and they were to land on Juno beach. Next was Major General Thomas Rennie, who was in command of the 3rd British Division, and they were to land on Sword beach, and the third was Major General Richard Gale, who was in command of the 6th Airborne Division. Our host, Major General D. A. H. Graham, was in command of the 50th British (Northumbrian) Division, and they were to land on Gold beach. The code name 'Gold beach', therefore, had a personal resonance for the General. I realised later that this explained his strange, faraway look when I had asked if a gold dress would be an appropriate colour to wear. Major General Gale only stayed for a very short time as he was due back to his camp for dinner. The other two stayed for a while longer.

When I searched my memory for the names of the officers I met that evening, many came to mind because of their association with colours, spelling or family names. Here is an example. Two officers came in together and walked smartly up to the General to report they had arrived. The first to be introduced was Lt Col R. A. Phayre, Commanding Officer for the 147th Field Regiment. On shaking his hand I queried, 'F-A-I-R?' He smiled and replied, 'No, P-H-A-Y-R-E.' I remarked, 'Such an unusual spelling, I shall never forget it.' The second officer was Lt Col A. E. Green, Commanding

Officer for the 6th Bn The Durham Light Infantry. To him I said, 'How strange, I shall never forget your name, as I have just met a Mr White and a Mr Black.' These were Lt Col G. W. White, Commanding Officer for the 5th Bn East Yorkshire Regiment and Lt Col T. J. Black, who was A.A. & Q.M.G. on the staff of General Graham. Colours being important in my line of expertise meant that these names were never forgotten.

Suddenly, Lt Col Green gave a violent shudder, which caused his colleague to ask, 'Are you all right?' He replied, 'Yes, just a chill. I'll be all right for the next few days.' This was the start of the attack of malaria that prevented him leading his troops on D-Day, for he was confined in hospital. His second in command, Major G. L. Wood, took over at very short notice. Other officers I remember meeting during the evening were:

Brigadier F. Y. C. Knox (C. O. 69th Infantry Brigade)
Brigadier C. H. Norton (C. O. Royal Artillery)
Brigadier R. H. Senior (C. O. 151st Infantry Brigade)
Brigadier Sir Alexander Stanier (C. O. 231st Infantry Brigade)
Lt Col R. H. W. S. Hastings (C. O. 6th Bn The Green Howards)
Lt Col S. V. Keeling (C. O. 2nd Bn The Cheshire Regiment)
Lt Col Sir William Mount (C. O. 61st Reconnaissance Regiment)
Lt Col C. A. R. Nevill (C. O. 2nd Bn The Devonshire Regiment.)
Lt Col E. H. M. Norie (C. O. 1st Bn The Dorsetshire Regiment)
Lt Col P. H. Richardson (C. O. 7th Bn The Green Howards)
Lt Col H. D. N. Smith (C.O. 1st Bn The Hampshire Regiment)

Others from the General's staff were Lt B. Henderson A. D. C., and Captain P. D. Crichton-Stuart, staff officer. As most of the officers were in mess uniform or in battledress, the appearance of the latter in full Scottish dress caused many to gasp at the sight. He gazed around in astonishment at his colleagues and said, 'I thought this was to be an occasion', which of course, it was.

When I spoke to Lt Mant, who was a liaison officer on the staff of General Graham, in August 1985, he said, 'Although I was not at the party, I heard on Sunday when on board HMS *Nitch* from Lt Col Norie what a good do it had been.'

Another officer brought in by the General was clearly very reluctant to stay for more than a few minutes and refused to take any refreshment. The General had to take him back to his billet. This officer was killed shortly after landing.

Several ladies in American uniform were engaged in dancing the jitterbug, but they did not stay longer than an hour or so. The General hurriedly excused himself from my side during this time to remove an American officer who had been overcome with emotion. He rapidly escorted him and his dance partner, Joy Cooke, out of the hut. She was not to be seen until some five days afterwards, and when I met her in the corridor Joy told me she had not been allowed out into the public area until that morning! It was part of my brief to cover any such incident and ensure the continuance of the social atmosphere.

By nine o'clock all the guests had arrived and I was able to relax. One officer asked if he could get me a drink and I asked for orangeade. Then another said, 'May I fetch you some food?' and from then on, a non-stop procession of courteous young men vied with each other to keep me supplied. I quickly organised a little of this and a little of that, keeping everyone happy, making sure they fed themselves at the same time.

Although I remained at the centre table, my companions changed frequently. The conversations that ensued varied in subject from places, holidays, gardens, flowers, trees and famous houses to visit, to music and musical concerts – such as those I had attended in Winchester given by Dame Myra Hess and Benno Moiseiwitsch. Photography was mentioned and I was handed a photograph of the wife and child of one of the officers. I remarked, 'Oh she is a charming little girl.' His neighbour slapped his hands on the table and stood up, saying, 'Excuse me' and slipping away, leaving everyone stunned into immobility. Pushing the photograph towards its owner, I suggested he put it back into his wallet.

This was one of the tricky situations which I had been forewarned could happen at any time during the evening. Somehow, I had to break the tension. So I started to talk about a visit to the National Gallery a few weeks before. By the time I had described some of the pictures they had all regained their composure. Asking, 'Has anyone visited the National Gallery or any other exhibition?' I got a response and soon they were talking normally again. What a relief.

Knowing nothing about regiments but recognising both Hampshire and Dorset badges, I enquired as to the Sphinx on it and the word Egypt. This would be a safe subject, and I was told a little of the regiment's history. Then, indicating a white double-headed cross on some of the uniforms, I remarked that it looked like the sword of retribution, similar to the cross of Lorraine. This caused many amused chuckles. My instinctive thought was that it could be a recognition sign for the invasion of France. Years later I was informed it was the badge of the Tyne and Tees, representing the three rivers, Tyne, Tees and Humber. The H is shown when the badge is turned on its side.

The General, having welcomed his guests, began to relax and asked if I would like to dance, and what my preference was. The request to the band for a waltz was given, and I think we gave a very creditable performance, as at the end applause accompanied us off the floor.

As the last guests were leaving the General said, 'I'm sorry, I shall have to ask you to wait for a while before I take you home because I must see all my men in bed before I leave. I hope you don't mind.' I assured him it did not matter what time I returned, as my landlady had given me a key. As everyone was scurrying about removing all the food, dishes, cloths and tables, I queried as to where I should wait as I did not want to be in the way. Finding a seat in the corner, he explained they had to clear the hut by midnight. He left saying, 'I will try not to be away too long.'

From chatting to the waiter who was clearing tables, I learned that earlier that day the General had returned from SHAEF HQ at 10 a.m. and instructed his staff to put into immediate action all arrangements for the party. Invitations were sent out to all Commanding Officers of the D-Day invasion and their staff. A few minutes later he had left the camp on his way to meet Joe Smith at Hursley Park House. From there he was taken through the grounds to the hanger, under its camouflaged net, to the office of Eric Lovell-Cooper, Chief Draughtsman of Vickers Supermarine.

Just before midnight the General returned carrying my jacket, and while I was putting it on, I heard him say to an officer, 'I am taking Miss Broughton home and you will be in charge while I am away. I will speak to all the guards on my way out.' Then, turning to the two MPs, he said, 'When everything has been cleared, lock up and you are free to go off duty.'

*

Outside, his jeep was waiting, with the driver who had brought me into camp earlier. I climbed into the rear seat, and the General got in beside me. It was a bumpy ride down through the forest, and I was glad of the support of his arm. At each gate he got out and spoke to the men on guard duty, giving them explicit instructions as to who was in charge while he was out of the camp. He reminded them to keep alert and on their toes. When we reached the main road the driver sped off in the direction of Winchester. To make conversation I remarked on how much organisation had gone into making the evening such a success. Then he said, 'I hope you were not too disturbed by the various incidents that happened.' 'Not at all,' I replied. 'Thank you for your instructions earlier, they helped me to cope when you were not around.'

In trying to reply, his voice broke, so when he asked, 'Do you mind if I put my arms round you?' I said, 'If you wish,' for I realised he was desperately fighting for control and needed the close human contact. As his arms came round, his head dropped on to my shoulder. His whole body was shaking and he held me as though he was clutching for dear life on to a lifebelt in the sea and I was his anchor. I must admit that for a moment I was shattered to feel the depth of the emotional outburst from this man who had in his command the lives of thousands of men.

Throughout the evening he had kept a cheerful countenance, seeing that everyone had what they needed. It was vitally necessary for him to release his internal turmoil so that he could face the coming days with confidence in his command. I was concerned that the driver should on no account become aware of his breakdown, so even though the noise of the jeep was considerable, I pulled his head into the collar of my jacket so that his deep shuddering sobs were muffled, and encouraged him to cry it out: 'Cry it out, hold on, hold on tight,' as one does instinctively to children to reassure them that it is all right to cry. Gradually, his heaving shoulders became still. He was so embarrassed to have lost his equilibrium, but I said, 'Take this comfort in the spirit in which it is given. I do understand the enormous strain you have been under. You needed to break the tension and it was best to be with me, for there is no one else to help you and I can be discreet.' During the rest of the journey we did not speak again, but I held him close to give him time to recover his composure.

As we approached Battery Hill I suggested he tell the driver to stop at the junction, so he could reverse ready to return while we walked the last 100 yards. I knew if the jeep drove into the close at that time of night it could wake everyone up, and too much notice would be taken by the neighbours. Silently we walked down the path, and as we turned into the close he put his arm round my waist and seemed reluctant to say goodbye. Suddenly I thought that I must not say goodbye – it would be too final. Clasping his hands within mine I whispered, 'I will not say goodbye but – au revoir.' I could say no more.

As I opened the gate he took a step forward. A look of query on his face gave me the feeling that it was only then that he realised I knew precisely what was going on. Would I divulge anything? Should he really let me go free into the public area with all the information I had acquired during the evening? I stepped back and looking straight into his eyes said, 'Don't worry. I won't say anything. My prayers go with you and all your men.' This seemed to reassure him as he stood tall in the moonlight – a veritable leader of men. Raising a hand in farewell, I walked to the door, feeling his eyes still upon me, but I did not look back – it would have been the wrong thing to do.

Quietly turning the key I stepped inside and bolted the door. Removing my shoes, I crept up the stairs and into my room. Standing at the open window I heard the jeep start up and draw away into the distance. The General was on course to continue the campaign.

It has not been an easy task for me to write down the experience of those hours. The remembrance of that time brings a lump to my throat which threatens to overcome my composure even as I write nearly fifty years later. But I have been persuaded to record this event because it is considered unique in military history.

*

The strain that I had held in check all evening could now surface, and I found that sitting on my bed I had to grab hold of the metal framework while I shook uncontrollably, letting the tension gradually ease from my body.

I memorised every detail and relived the enormity of what I had witnessed. I recalled the names of the officers, their regiments, all the code words and some of the conversations. My thoughts turned into prayers for their safety in the days to come and for the man who was to lead them. He had cared for them so intensely that day, with no thought for his own comfort. I hoped that my support had done all that could have been done.

It was not until I had reviewed everything that had happened that I could release my grip and push all the knowledge into my subconscious, knowing it had to be forgotten for the time being. When writing this book I allowed the memories of this time to surface, and they came flooding back as fresh as if they had just occurred.

*

On waking up, I was horrified to view my face in the mirror. I looked years older, with shadowed eyes and pale complexion. After applying some careful makeup I began to look more like myself, but I could not do anything about my lack of energy.

Downstairs the boys had gone out and their grandmother was busy in the kitchen. Mrs Ward asked if I had enjoyed the evening, and I suddenly realised I would have to cover remarks about the party. All I could think of to say was that there was dancing and some wonderful food.

Aware that I could not face any further questions, there was only one thing to do. Pack a picnic lunch, get on my bike and disappear for the rest of the day. I crossed the main road and took a country lane due west into the open countryside for some 10 miles, to the memorial obelisk of a horse called Farley Mount. This pyramidal monument was erected by Mr Paulet St John in memory of his horse which, in September 1733, leapt into a chalk pit 25 feet deep when out fox hunting. In October 1734 they won the Hunter's Plate on Worthy Downs. The horse had been entered in the name of 'Beware Chalk Pit'.

No one could approach without due warning. My brain felt numb. The physical effort of cycling coupled with the warmth of the sun enabled me to relax, and for most of the day I dozed. Although I tried to read a book, my thoughts kept turning to the enormous undertaking of the assembly of the invasion forces.

What was likely to happen at work the next day? How was I to evade any questioning? Thinking this over, the answer seemed to be food. I could describe the buffet with genuine excitement, toss in the dancing and people would be satisfied. This would be my gambit for the day. After all, no one else would know of the many different units who were there. For all they knew it was just a camp of British and

American troops. Returning to my digs I went to bed, relatively hopeful that I had prepared myself for the next day, and I slept soundly.

*

Sure enough, back at work on Monday morning my colleagues were quite satisfied with my description of the food. But, as is often the case, there was a snag. One man from another section, I think he was something to do with a union, was persistent in his questions about Joy, the only other English girl at the party. 'Where was she? Why wasn't she at work?' I suggested that she probably had a hangover and had stayed in bed.

The next day he accosted me again, saying, 'She is not at work, not at home, and her parents don't know where she is.' Knowing full well why she was not around, I had to stop his meddling in this matter. I said, 'I cannot tell you, as I don't even know her or her family.' My obvious air of aloofness finally persuaded him to leave me alone. I imagine that when she appeared some days later he had to drop his sleuthing.

All that day I was on tenterhooks waiting for the announcement of the landings. At lunchtime I listened to the news on Gerry's radio, but there was no indication of an invasion. By mid-afternoon my hands had started to shake and I could not hold my pen steady. Was it possible the landings had been aborted or, had the invasion failed? Obviously I was in shock, and it was imperative that no one noticed my predicament. With only two hours to go I would cope. Going to Gerry, I quietly told him that I could not work. His immediate reaction was to send me home, but I said, 'Please don't make any fuss. I will be alright after tea. Please cover me and keep anyone away who may start asking questions.' He was puzzled, but agreed to my request.

That evening there was still nothing on the nine o'clock news. A quarter of an hour later, when we were playing a game of cards, we heard the steady rumble of aircraft. Mrs Ward exclaimed, 'We didn't miss the warning, did we?' Grandmother hurried into the kitchen and then called out, 'Come and look! There are lights in the sky!' Everyone scrambled down from the table and out of the back door to see a magnificent sight.

Over Winchester, three separate columns of aircraft were converging into one line. Group formations of layer upon layer of aircraft towing gliders followed, reaching up into the night sky. Their red and green wing-tip lights were so close they appeared to touch. Wave upon wave passed by us, barely 200 feet above, to follow the valley towards the coast and France. It was a glorious and heart-stopping vision. The invasion was ON!

Indoors I allowed Mrs Ward to know that what we had just witnessed was the reason why I had had to get away from everyone on Sunday. She was so relieved; she had been keeping a wary eye on me as my appetite had suddenly lessened. I was confident of her discretion because I knew she had signed the Official Secrets Act.

My memory of that evening is best described in the first paragraph of an article written by me which was published by Southern Tourist Board and Normandy Tourist Board in November 1993 in the *Travel, Trade and Veterans Newsletter*:

The relief felt on seeing the aircraft and gliders forming up a few hundred feet above Winchester, all navigation lights on, wing tip to wing tip and stacked in columns reaching high into the night sky.

Anyone who has seen the film *Close Encounters of the Third Kind* will have experienced a similar sound at the approach of the spacecraft. The pulsating rhythm of their engines was thunderous. David, Mrs Ward's eldest son, who was twelve years old at the time, recollected witnessing that evening's unique activity when I met him recently.

Special D-Day message from the Divisional Commander to all ranks of the 50th Northumbrian Division

The time is at hand to strike – to break through the Western Wall and into the Continent of Europe.

To you, officers and men of the 50th (Northumbrian) Division, has been given the great honour of being in the vanguard of this mighty blow for freedom.

It is my unshakable belief that we, together with Force 'G' of the Royal Navy, the special regiments of the Royal Armoured Corps, the Royal Artillery and the Royal Engineers attached to us and with the help of the RAF and American Air Force, will deliver such an overpowering punch that the enemy will be unable to recover. Thus shall we be well set to carry through to a glorious and successful end all that is now entrusted to us.

Much has been asked of you in the past and great have been your achievements, but this will be the greatest adventure of all. It will add yet another fine chapter to your already long and distinguished record – the grandest chapter of all.

Very best of luck to every one of you.

D. A. H. Graham, Major-General, Commander, 50th
(Northumbrian) Division

*

Peggy Richards, who was a VAD (Voluntary Aid Detachment), gave me the following story about the Royal Naval Hospital at Haslar, Gosport.

It was D-Day, we all knew what was happening and I shall never forget the awful sick feeling of apprehension while we waited. A month before, Haslar had evacuated all but a couple of patients who were too ill to be moved. Some of our laboratory SBAs (Service Blood Assistants) had vanished to the Naval laboratories at Cleveden to prepare the new drug, penicillin, in readiness for the arrival of casualties. We had been given our specific instructions and stations of duty for when 'IT' happened.

Travel was restricted, for we were 'sealed in' on the South Coast, and we watched the arrival of men, vehicles and guns. On every spare patch of ground, Army vehicles and equipment were packed so closely it seemed impossible to walk between them. Local buses had to stop halfway down Gosport High Street as the bus station at the harbour was taken over by tanks and lorries. The ferry, which normally took a few minutes to get to Portsmouth, now took two hours because of the increased Naval traffic.

Inside the hospital we turned two ground-floor wards into resuscitation units for those needing blood transfusions before operations. In the meantime we packed drums with sterilised dressings and filled hundreds of blood 'giving' sets.

Inside the wall of Haslar there was a raised hump with a seat, called the Admiral's Seat. From there you could see across the Solent to the Isle of Wight. In the evening standing there you felt you could have walked across to the island, if not to France, on decks of the hundreds of ships assembled in the Solent. Later a pilot wrote that from the air it looked as if the island was being towed out to sea. We sent our thoughts to the men and crews on board, silently wishing them 'God speed', and wondered how long it would be before some of them came back to Haslar.

At dawn we woke to see the Solent grey, empty and waiting. The silence was uncanny. A frightening anticipation of what was to come. From midday on Wednesday the main stream of casualties began to come in. None of us could have envisaged what the next days and weeks would bring. The endless stream of ambulances, the filthy soaking clothing piled in the sluices, bathrooms and even in the corridors as the underground operating theatres worked day and night, around the clock. The stench of the terrible wounds we would dress as we would try and comfort the dying.

The casualty department received the wounded as they arrived, and their immediate needs were dealt with. Each VAD on duty was given cigarettes, and to hold one for a puff was all we could do for some of them. In the wards their filthy uniforms were removed and they were cleaned up prior to theatre. By the next day many were on their way up north to safer areas, or to specialised hospitals such as East Grinstead for burns, in order to free their beds for those wounded who were still coming in. There was no leave for staff for over three weeks, and our precious three hours off duty was frequently cancelled.

The tenderness shown by the SBAs to those wounded who were unlikely to live will never be forgotten. In the blackout an SBPO (Service Blood Programme Officer) would play the organ in the church, giving us the comfort and strength to face the next day of horror.

The description by Helen Long in her book *Change into Uniform* gives another description of that time.

> Viewed from Haslar, the armada was laid out as it were on a stage beneath the hospital walls ... Suddenly there they all were! Above floated a haze of silver balloons attached by gossamer threads to armed merchant cruisers, corvettes, trawlers, minesweepers, destroyers, tank landing craft, M.T.B.s, M.L.s, and ocean going tugs. Each one proudly holding, like a child at a party, its portly balloon. On the top floor a VAD glanced out of the window and saw below, a grey sea, grey not with sea but with ships ... They formed a solid mass whose limits were beyond her vision. Later that afternoon a rating also looked out but moved quickly away and he too said nothing. This was how everyone kept silent.

*

My search for any of the commanding officers who attended the farewell party on Saturday 3 June 1944, hosted by Major General D. A. H. Graham, took several years. Eventually I found a person in Scotland of one of the same unusual surnames as I had remembered from the party. I was given the telephone number of his cousin. To my delight he proved to be Lieutenant Colonel R. A. Phayre, Commanding Officer of the 147th Field Regiment R. A., who had been present at the party. Now retired as brigadier, he lived in Camberley, Surrey. His letter to me of November 1992 recalled his memory of that occasion and our conversation regarding the spelling of his name. He also remembered other officers were Lt Col 'Cosmo' Nevill of the 2nd Devonshires, and Brigadier Sir Alex Stanier, Commanding Officer of the 231st Brigade. He continued with his recollections of D-Day as follows:

> On Sunday June 4 1944 I joined Brigadier Stanier with a small staff to embark in HMS *Nitch* at Southampton for our one-way trip to Normandy. We changed into a landing craft from HMS *Nitch* some 10 miles from the beach. Close to the shore we were sunk by a mine, and had to wade, waist high in rough water. We established a temporary HQ by the sea wall, and I was responsible for controlling the artillery fire in support of the units of 231st Brigade Group. These harrowing memories are very painful. Some months later, before the crossing of the Rhine, when the 8th Armoured Brigade – of which the Essex Yeomanry were part – were in support of the 31st Highland Division, General Rennie, the GOC, invited commanding officers to the 'last supper', which was sadly very appropriate as he and his C. R. A. Brigadier Shiel were killed the next day.

I am extremely sorry not to have been able to visit and accept his invitation to lunch, as he developed bronchitis and died shortly after writing to me. The brigadier's cousin and wife kindly invited me to spend a week with them to research places and buildings relating to my family. They were most helpful and I particularly appreciated his criticism of my first attempts at writing episodes for my book.

*

In 1995 Colonel Brownrigg sent me his thoughts for inclusion in this book, relating to the time when he was a major and second in command of the 61st Reconnaissance Regiment. I am indebted to him for his insight into the character of his divisional commander.

Lieutenant Colonel Sir William Mount, Commanding Officer of the 61st Reconnaissance Regiment, was wounded on D-Day 2, and as his second in command I took over temporarily. Every evening I used to go to see General Graham at Divisional Headquarters to report on the day's work. Two days later he said he was arranging for me to take over the command, officially. This made me warm to him, as there was a pool of lieutenant colonels waiting to take over the command of battalions or regiments that had lost their commanding officers.

Earlier, when the Normandy campaign had become virtually static, General Graham put each of the three squadrons under the command of his three brigade commanders. This did not work well in my view. I suggested that the squadrons should be under my command, but individually 'in support of' the three brigades, so that I was consulted over the tasks they were given. He considered this idea and said, 'All right, we will give that a trial and see if it works.' And happily it did. Later on, when the advance really began, we worked together as a regiment. He was always friendly and I never recall his once offering a sharp word, except to his ADC, saying, 'Can't you see Colonel Brownrigg's had a hard day? Get him a cup of tea quickly.' And even that was said in a gentle way.

The informal efficiency of the Divisional Headquarters was superb. One day during the Normandy campaign our intelligence sergeant went to get the latest 'picture' from Divisional Headquarters instead of from the intelligence office. As he was walking over to the intelligence map the divisional commander saw his black beret from his caravan and called out 'Hello, Recce*! What do you want?' When he heard, he said, 'Come in here, I'll show you what's happening. They don't know anything over there.' Was it any wonder that the General's visits to the regiment were always immensely popular? Sadly, General Graham had a nasty fall from his caravan towards the end of 1944 and had to give up command of the 50th Division.

* Recce – short for Reconnaissance.

Soon after, he wrote to me thus:

'Will you tell all your officers and men how grateful I am for all the grand work they have done. They have been simply magnificent and although their battle history is not long as time goes, it has been a glorious one and every one of you can feel justifiably proud of all you have achieved. When much that has happened in this war is forgotten, the memory of your deeds will remain. My heartfelt thanks to you, one and all.'

We were indeed fortunate to serve under the command of such a great General and a wonderful character.

Signed,

Philip Brownrigg

8

AFTER THE WAR

When the Second World War ended, my work for Supermarine was gradually being superseded by photography so I was prevailed upon to return home to assist Mother, who had not been in good health. Father had arranged a part-time job for me as a clerk running the 'shop' in the college. This, along with coping with cleaning the house and doing the laundry and the garden, kept me fully occupied. I felt rather bored, but looking forward to my marriage kept me going. Back home in my old haunts I missed the companionship of my cat Jinky. Before I went to college he had been put to sleep.

On a visit to Purbrook School I was impressed by the alterations which had taken place over the years. I missed the weeping copper beech: our famous tree, which had been such a focal point, had unfortunately been cut down. After 200 years the first stone step of the main stairs had worn very thin. A photograph records the fact that I was privileged to be the first person allowed to step on these after the treads had been resurfaced.

Yalta: Spitfire Presentation Book

When Churchill was to meet Roosevelt and Stalin at Yalta in 1945, the powers that be thought it would be a gesture of goodwill to give them each a book on the Spitfire. It was quarto sized, with single pages depicting each Mark with Merlin engines. The top half of each page had a simple perspective drawing (most of them done by myself) and Gerry Gingell had written the basic details on the lower half. Six copies were made; two were bound in red leather to be presented to Roosevelt and Stalin, four others were bound in blue leather, one of which was for Churchill.

On a visit to my local library I found a book which showed a print of a photograph designated to the Imperial War Museum. It showed Stalin cradling a quarto book on his knees, and Churchill was holding another down by his side. The photograph was obviously taken towards the end of the evening, as both were in informal dress without hats and beaming broadly at the photographer.

Unfortunately I did not take the name of the book or its author, and when I returned to the library it had been removed from their stock. Enquiries at the Imperial War Museum proved unsuccessful, for the photograph seems to have disappeared. This has been one of my few unsuccessful searches. If by any chance this photograph is familiar to anybody, or if the whereabouts of one of the Spitfire Presentation Books is known, I would dearly like to hear.

Tea with Field Marshal Montgomery

In the summer of 1962, my husband, having only recently passed his driving test, requested me to navigate the cross-country journey to visit Field Marshal Montgomery at Isington Mill in Alton. I remained in the car reading a book, believing my husband to be busy for at least a couple of hours. After a few minutes he returned, saying the Field Marshal had spotted me and told him not to leave his wife outside but to bring her in. My husband was insistent that I should not discuss the war with him.

On approaching the main door I noticed a very large millstone was used as a step, with smaller stones laid beside the path, making a feature of the entrance. Having settled my husband to his work, the Field Marshal indicated that we should take a walk round his garden. Stepping on to the lawn, I was dubious about leaving holes in the finely cut turf as I was wearing high-heeled shoes. Drawing his attention to this fact, he quickly assured me it was not a problem as 'the gardener mows the centre circle every day, the surrounding 2 feet every two days and the outer edges once a week.' No wonder everything looked so trim; even the willows, not yet in leaf, marched in ranks along the river edge. At the far end, where the mill race parted from the River Wey, we discussed what other plants that required little maintenance could be used. Having planted *Cornus alba* the previous year in our garden I was able to suggest these could be interspersed so that the vibrant red stems would complement the yellow of his willows. On later reading the book written by his brother, I noted that my suggestion had been implemented.

Our conversation continued on the subject of art. Mentioning that he had received several amateur portraits of himself, he thought it would interest me to see them, and we went indoors. Walking into the entrance hall, he commented on the fact that the floors were made of Tasmanian oak. The cedar shingles on the barns came from Canada, and the mountain ash had come from Victoria. All these woods had been presented to him. On the stairs up to the landing, several oil paintings were hung along the wall. I gave each but a cursory glance as we walked along, for they were not to my taste. At the end he spun round and said, 'Now. Give me your opinion of these portraits.' Startled at his request, I was jolted into a considered re-appraisal. My first reaction had noted the vulgar colours and treatment of the subject. Giving all of them a second look, I strove to define one item on which I could make a positive comment. Fortunately, I found one had captured the tilt of the head, another the definition of the eyes, yet another the set of an ear and one in which the use of a softer palette gave a gentler mood. He was pleased at my remarks and nodded in agreement. Then, taking me by the hand, he drew me towards his bedroom saying, in a conspiratorial tone, 'Come and look at the only one I can live with.' Skirting the end of the four-poster bed, he pointed to another painting hung on the far wall. It was less vibrant and less aggressive in treatment and a much better likeness – I had to agree it was the best of the bunch.

Moving away, my attention was caught by two portraits that hung over the bed-head. The left-hand one I recognised as that of his father, the large painting of whom I had observed in the dining hall before climbing the stairs. The other was of Pope Pius XII. Seeing that I looked puzzled because I knew he was a staunch supporter of the Church of England, he commented, 'Both men have been my great inspiration.'

Returning downstairs to the hall, he proceeded to show me the beautiful collection of silver items that had been presented to him. I was very impressed by his field marshal's baton, which lay in a velvet-lined case. The 'salt' had pride of place on the dining table, which had been set for tea. Years later I was very saddened to hear of a burglary in which he lost all of these items. Could they not at least have left his baton?

My husband, having finished his assignment, joined us and the housekeeper brought in the tea tray. After a short grace, the Field

Marshal turned the tea tray towards me, saying, 'Stella, will you be mother?' After tea, when my husband was out of the hall, I was much amused by his pointing to a dish of fruit and saying, 'Do have a 'nana'. He explained with a smile, 'That's what I call them to the children.' He then told me that he was in the process of writing his memoirs. At this juncture I felt compelled to let him know of my work with Supermarine and my maiden name.

The instant he heard it his eyes lit up and, leaning towards me with an upraised finger, said, 'Ah! Then you must be the young lady who was with Graham.' I smiled and nodded, because we could not say anything further as my husband had come back into the hall. I knew he had recalled the situation in which I had been involved on the evening before D-Day, for he had to give permission for me to be there. How I wished we could have met again – but it was not to be.

Supermariners and the Spitfire Society

At Rothsay College in Bedford I met Squadron Leader Ian Blair. On a visit with him to the Royal Air Force Museum (Hendon) he drew my attention to a poster. It depicted an RAF youth with the words 'Careless talk may cost his life' and underneath it was the instruction 'Don't talk about Aerodromes or Aircraft Factories'. The youth was Ian. On the 4 September 1940 Ian, as an observer in a Blenheim flying in the Middle East Command, took over the controls when the pilot was killed. Without previous flying experience he flew the aircraft 350 miles back to safety, thereby saving the lives of the air gunner and himself, plus the Blenheim. For this he was awarded the Distinguished Flying Medal.

Hearing that Jack Davis was to give the thirtieth R. J. Mitchell Memorial Lecture on 4 March 1986, entitled 'The Basic Design of the Prototype Spitfire', in the Bolderwood lecture theatre of the University of Southampton, I mentioned it to Ian. As he was interested, we went down together. After the lecture I saw Alan Clifton and spoke to him. He immediately turned to Jeffery Quill with the remark, 'Jeffery, you remember Stella?' It was great to speak with them and to reminisce with Jack Davis and others of our memories of Hursley Park.

On the following day Ian took me to Eastleigh Airport, where the recently formed Spitfire Society was holding a 'Spitfire Fly-In'. This was the golden jubilee of the first flight of the prototype Spitfire on 5 March 1936 from the aerodrome.

The Spitfire Society was inaugurated on 6 March 1984 at the Royal Air Force Museum (Hendon), under Jeffrey Quill as President and Group Captain David Green as Chairman. On 26 May 1984 the R. J. Mitchell Memorial Museum was opened in the Southampton Hall of Aviation.

At Eastleigh I met Mike Baylis, a professional photographer who was taking photographs of various groups. Ian was delighted to meet his colleagues of the 602 Squadron of the Tangmere Spitfire Wing, namely Michael Frances, Raymond Baxter and Michael Penny. Some forty-six Supermariners were also at this celebration, and photographs of both these groups were produced in the souvenir edition of the Spitfire Society's golden jubilee magazine. The magazine was originally entitled *D.C.O.* (Duty Carried Out), but since autumn 2003 it has been renamed *Spitfire*. Nick Grace's Spitfire trainer had landed on grass at the end of the runway when the undercarriage collapsed and it tipped over on its nose. Peter Arnold, Spitfire historian, and Henri de Meer were to have flown this aircraft, but had to resign themselves to the fact that their flight was cancelled. Also on that day I met Noel Mills and his wife Joan. Noel recalled the 'sports day' when we were roped in at the last minute to take part in a three-legged race representing the Drawing Office against the house team. We came in second, which was not bad considering we had had no time for rehearsal.

At the Hall of Aviation in Southampton on another occasion I was delighted to meet with Jack Rasmussen and Kenneth Knell, both Supermariners, with their wives. Dr Gordon Mitchell, son of R. J. Mitchell, the famous designer of the Spitfire, was also there, and Miss Lettice Curtis. She was one of the female ferry pilots during the war and now was a vice-president of the Spitfire Society. Meeting with Jeffrey and other Supermarine colleagues after forty years felt like greeting long-lost members of a family.

Jeffrey proposed I should become a life member of the Spitfire Society, and 'being a person with the required proven connections', the committee elected me on 11 November 1985. I was then persuaded to become Chairman of one of the eight regions, namely the Central Region covering London to Peterborough.

Throughout the next four years I organised the Central Region's stands at various air shows. This activity was supported by a committee of Spitfire enthusiasts of varying ages, who gave of their time and energy to attend these functions in order to raise funds and interest the general public in the society. Having no transport of my own, I am very grateful to members who made sure that the tent, sales items and myself were able to be present at air shows throughout the region. The membership steadily increased and contacts were made in many countries.

At one air show I was approached by a German, who diffidently asked if it would be acceptable for him and his colleagues,

Luftwaffe pilots, to meet with the Spitfire pilots who were signing posters on our stand. Checking that everyone was happy about meeting the Luftwaffe pilots, I introduced the two parties. A unique experience for all.

This was all hard work, and after four years of meeting pilots who flew Spitfires, Seafires and the ferry pilots, plus many Supermariners, I felt I had made a good contribution to the establishment of the society. It had been a very busy time, and when I developed ME and had to give it up, I concentrated on the research and writing of this book. Since then I have been most fortunate in having been able to contact many surviving colleagues of that time.

At the RAF Club in Piccadilly on Thursday 12 December 1991 Jeffrey Quill was presented with a trophy by the Chief of the Air Staff. Many of our wartime colleagues were present. In conversation with Jeffrey and Jack Rasmussen, I said it would be helpful if a book could be compiled listing the names of the design staff who had been involved in the development of the Spitfire, and that Gerry Gingell would probably be the best source of information. My remarks obviously gave Jeffrey food for thought, because he later discussed the idea with Gerry.

At the Southampton Hall of Aviation on Thursday 8 May 1997, the Supermarine Spitfire Memorial Book, proposed by Jeffrey Quill and compiled by Gerry Gingell and colleagues, sponsored by Messier-Dowty and Dowty Aerospace, was presented to the director of the R. J. Mitchell Memorial Museum by Alex Henshaw. This hand-made edition records as many names as possible of those who were involved in the original design and subsequent development of the Spitfire from 1932 to 1945 under R. J. Mitchell and later Joseph Smith. Two other hand-made books have been presented to the Royal Air Force Museum (Hendon) and Imperial War Museum (Duxford). Copies of this book were given to other dignitaries. The Southampton *Daily Echo* reported this occasion and photographed most of the thirty-six members of Supermarine who were present. Jeffrey, who was to have been the principal guest, had, regretfully, died a few days earlier.

Watching a programme about art on the television in the 1990s I saw two people walking away from the camera. There was no mistaking one of them. His distinctive walk was that of Ken Sprague, a colleague at Supermarine. Looking through pages of my autograph album, I found his colourful entry. After making some telephone calls I got in touch with him, hoping he would be able to be at the next reunion. Unfortunately this was not possible, but on the day he rang me at the venue and Gerry was able to chat with him. When staying near Exeter some years ago I took the opportunity to meet him, as he was in Exeter Hospital overnight. His comment to his surgeon and the people in the ward was 'Can you believe it! We worked together sixty years ago!' And he illustrated another picture opposite the one in my album.

At meetings of the Central Region we were very honoured to have prestigious speakers such as Sir Rex Hunt, the former Governor of the Falkland Islands, and Air Marshal Sir Ivor Broom, former President of the Pathfinder Association. The latter became a close friend and learned of my involvement with General Graham and the D-Day commanders. Hearing that an officer who was present at the farewell party had written to me and confirmed my presence, he persuaded me to record my memories, as 'it was such a unique episode in the annals of military history'.

During the Second World War, as a civilian, I was privileged to have played a small part in all three sections of our armed forces, to have worked alongside many men who gave their energy and expertise in many fields and to succeed in setting free the peoples of Europe from the Nazi programme and the dictatorship of Adolf Hitler.

BIBLIOGRAPHY

Barnes, Barrie S., *The Sign of the Double 'T'* (Sentinel Publishing, 1999).

Belcham, Major General David, *All in the Day's March* (Collins, 1978).

Belcham, Major General David, *Victory in Normandy*, (Chatto & Windus, 1981).

Bradley, General Omar, *A General's Life* (Simon & Schuster, 1983).

Bradley, General Omar, *A Soldier's Story* (Henry Holt & Co., 1951).

Bredin, Major A.E.C., *Three Assault Landings* (Gale & Polden, 1946).

Burton, Lesley, *D-Day: Our Great Enterprise* (Gosport Society, 1984).

Clay, Major Ewart W., *The Path of the 50th* (Gale & Polden, 1950).

Curtis, Lettice, *The Forgotten Pilots* (G. T. Foulis & Co. Ltd, 1971).

D.C.O., now *SPITFIRE*, Spitfire Society.

D-Day: 50th Anniversary of the Normandy Landings (Southern Newspapers, 1944).

Dunphie, Christopher and Garry Johnson, *Gold Beach* (Pen & Sword, 1999).

Ellis, L. F. et al., *Victory in the West: Volume 1, The Battle of Normandy* (Naval and Military Press, 2009).

English, Major Ian, *The Sign of the Double T* (Sentinel Publishing, 1999).

Griffiths, Harry, *Testing Times* (United Writers Publications, 1992).

Hamilton, Nigel, *Monty*, Vol. 2 (Hamish Hamilton Ltd, 1983).

Henshaw, Alex, *Sigh for a Merlin* (Crecy Publishing, 1999).

Horne, Alistair, *The Lonely Leader* (Pan, 2002).

Kee, Robert, *1945: The World We Fought For* (Penguin Books, 1995).

Long, Helen, *Change into Uniform* (Terence Dalton Ltd, 1971).

Mason, Francis K., *Battle over Britain* (McWhirter Twins Ltd, 1969).

McElwee, William, *The Battle of D Day* (Faber, 1965).

Montgomery, Brian, *A Field Marshal in the Family* (Pen & Sword Military, 2010).

Morgan and Shacklady, *Spitfire* (Key Books Ltd, 2000)

Moses, Harry, *The Faithful Sixth: A History of the Sixth Battalion, Durham Light Infantry* (Memoir Club, 2012).

Neillands, Robin, *D-Day, 1944: Voices from Normandy* (Motorbooks International, 1944).

Peacock, Lady, *Field Marshal the Viscount Montgomery: His Life* (Hutchinson, 1951).

Price, Alfred, *The Spitfire Story* (J. H. Haynes & Co. Ltd, 2010).

Quill, Jeffrey, *Spitfire: A Test Pilot's Story* (Crecy Publishing, 1998).

Ryan, Cornelius, *The Longest Day: The Classic Epic of D-Day, June 6 1944* (Simon & Schuster, 1994).

Scarfe, Norman, *Assault Division* (Spellmount, 2006).

Spooner, Tony, *Clean Sweep* (Goodall Publications Ltd, 2001).

Travel & Trade & Veterans Newsletter (Southern & Normandy Tourist Boards, November 1993, Issue 3).

Trew, Simon, *Gold Beach* (Sutton Publishing, 2004)

Warner, Philip, *The Daily Telegraph Book of the D Day Landings* (Leo Cooper Ltd, 2004).

Wheatley, Dennis, *The Deception Planners* (Hutchinson, 1980).

Wills, Henry, *Pillboxes* (Leo Cooper, 1985).

Winterbotham, F. W., *The Ultra Secret* (Dell, 1975).

Young, Irene, *Enigma Variations* (Mainstream Publishing, 2000).

INDEX

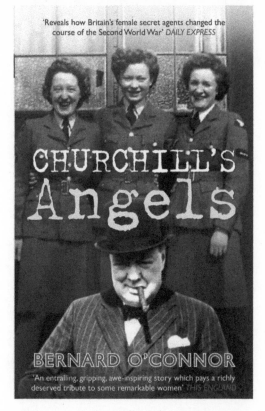

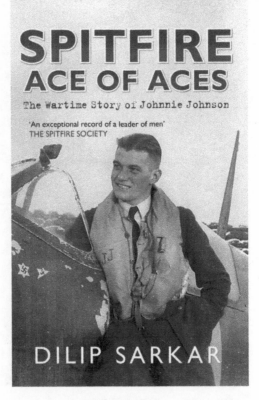

Also available from Amberley Publishing

How to fly the legendary fighter plane in combat using the manuals and instructions supplied by the RAF during the Second World War

'A Must' *INTERCOM: THE AIRCREW ASSOCIATION*

An amazing array of leaflets, books and manuals were issued by the War Office during the Second World War to aid pilots in flying the Supermarine Spitfire, here for the first time they are collated into a single book with the original 1940s setting. An introduction is supplied by expert aviation historian Dilip Sarkar. Other sections include aircraft recognition, how to act as an RAF officer, bailing out etc.

£9.99 Paperback
40 illustrations
264 pages
978-1-84868-436-2

Available from all good bookshops or to order direct
Please call **01453-847-800**
www.amberley-books.com